DO YOU KNOW WHO YOU ARE?

DO YOU KNOW WHO YOU ARE?

Discover the real you

Megan Kaye

LONDON, NEW YORK, MUNICH, MELBOURNE, AND DELHI

Author: Megan Kaye
Consultant: Joannah Ginsburg, LCSW

Editor: Allison Singer
Senior Designer: Collette Sadler
Designers: Mandy Earey, Saskia Janssen,
Jessica Lee, Charlotte Seymour
Design Assistant: Kate Fenton
Managing Editor: Dawn Henderson
Managing Art Editor: Christine Keilty
Senior Jacket Creative: Nicola Powling
Pre-Production Producer: Andy Hilliard
Senior Production Controller: Oliver Jeffreys
Creative Technical Support: Sonia Charbonnier
Editorial Director: Nancy Ellwood
Art Director: Peter Luff
Publisher: Peggy Vance

First published in Great Britain in 2014 by
Dorling Kindersley Limited
80 Strand
London WC2R 0RL

2 4 6 8 10 9 7 5 3
006—196501—Aug/14

A CIP catalogue record for this book is available from the British Library.

ISBN 978-1-4093-4838-2

Printed and bount in China by Hung Hing

Discover more at
www.dk.com

Contents

Introduction

Who are you? It's probably the single most important question you'll ever have to answer. The quest for self-knowledge is one that intrigues everyone, from sages to celebs. Your self, after all, is the lens through which you see the world and the face you present to it. If you don't know who you are, it can be difficult to know where you stand. Having a good grasp on your own thoughts, feelings, and personality is the starting point for getting a grip on everything else.

But which version of you is the **real** you? Is it the version you are when you're alone, when you're with your closest friends, when you're with your family? Is it the version you are at school, on the web, on a date, at a concert? **Life can be complicated,** and identity is a changeable thing. Ask yourself **"Who am I?"** and you can come up with a thousand different answers.

Well, we didn't have space in this book for a thousand different pages, but we do have a lot of **questionnaires, tests, quizzes, writing activities,** and **thought experiments** to help you get started. There's no particular right way to read this book; you can start at the beginning and work your way to the end, you can flip through and settle on whatever you're interested in at the moment, or, if you're feeling **daring**, you can just open to a page at random. You can take the quizzes solo, thinking carefully about what the questions mean to you, or you can do them with friends and family for added fun. Just like there's no one way to be a great person, there's no one way to read this book. It's all about finding your **personal style.**

Too many personality tests are written with only one good outcome. (It's "Goldilocks and the Three Bears" syndrome: if you get result A, you're too this! If you get result C, you're too that! But if you get result B, you can relax, you're just right.) We all know **that's not how life really works,** so rather than set irritating traps like that, the quizzes here have a variety of good and not-so-good outcomes. Almost every outcome has its **pros and cons,** because every kind of personality does. The aim is to figure out **who you are,** not to double-check whether you are **who you "should" be.** Whoever you are, there are ways of being the best, happiest, nicest, and smartest version of that.

Some of these quizzes are based on the work of real psychologists and others are **lighthearted fun;** some of them have answers to pick that'll lead you to a choice of outcomes, and others are more exploratory, acting as guides to help you work out for yourself what you think about things. (And, hey, which type of quiz you prefer probably tells you something about yourself, too.)

So, are you the same person now that you were in the past? Who do you think you'll be in the future? Really, **who are you?** Turn the page to start answering that all-important question. Or, you know, don't: flip to a random page in the middle of the book, or pass it to your best friend, or retreat to your bedroom and open it carefully at your desk, or curl up with it under your covers. The choice, like every other choice you'll find in this book, **is up to you.**

Five Factor Test

If you've ever wondered, **"What's my personality like?"** another question should immediately pop up: what does "personality" even mean anyway? It's a big question that keeps psychiatrists and psychologists busy. This Five Factor test, also known as the "Big Five" test, is an absolute classic on the subject.

The basic concept is this:

Personality traits aren't so much an either/or as they are a sliding scale – nobody's entirely mean or entirely nice, and nobody's totally stable or totally careless. Instead, we tend to lean more towards one extreme than the other. The idea behind the "Big Five" test is to see where you place yourself on the scale between extremes. So, take a look at these five sections and see where you land on the scale for each.

Section One

- New ideas get me excited. ○
- Art matters to me a lot. ○
- I've got a rich vocabulary and I like to use it. ○
- Abstract concepts appeal to me. ○
- I like to use my imagination. ○
- I can really get into a theoretical conversation. ○

Give yourself a score of 1 to 5 depending on how much each statement applies to you:

① = Pretty much never
② = Not really
③ = Sometimes yes, sometimes no
④ = Yes, probably
⑤ = Definitely

Next, add up your score for each section, then turn the page to analyse your answers. If you get a score of less than 6 or more than 30 for any section, you probably need to check your maths; a score of 18 places you right in the middle.

Section Three

- I like meeting new people every chance I get. ○
- I'm the life of the party. ○
- I'm often the one who starts a conversation. ○
- It's really easy to get to know me. ○
- I'm a fast-talker, not a ponderer. ○
- I enjoy being the centre of attention. ○

Section Two

- I make plans and I stick to them. ○
- I'm usually well prepared for things. ○
- I'm a self-starter. ○
- I like to make sure I clean up after myself. ○
- If it has to be done, I won't try to get out of it. ○
- I pay close attention to detail. ○

Section Five

- I pretty much accept people for who they are. ○
- I'll take time to help people out. ○
- I like to make other people feel at ease. ○
- I try to put things gently. ○
- I'd rather forgive and forget than hold a grudge. ○
- I take on other people's problems as my own. ○

Section Four

- I'm pretty hard on myself most of the time. ○
- It's not difficult to stress me out. ○
- I often feel threatened. ○
- I don't find it that easy to relax. ○
- I frequently get the blues. ○
- If someone does me wrong, I can get pretty angry. ○

Turn the page for analysis... ➤

< Five Factor Test *results*

Section One Total: ....

Section Two Total: ....

Section Three Total: ....

Section Four Total: ....

Section Five Total: ....

Section One
measures your openness to experience.

Some people are **adventurers,** whether in actual travel or in the world of **ideas** and **emotions;** they like variety and tend to be creative. Other people prefer routine and familiarity – the **tried and tested.** The scale is between **curiosity and caution;** a higher score means you're more open to new things, while a lower score means you like what you already know. Of course, this is all subject to circumstance: if you're living under a lot of **stress,** for instance, you might be more **cautious** because more's at stake. If your life is **normal and calm,** you might feel safe going off exploring, and you may crave **stimulation.** There's a strong pull between the two extremes – when the world opens up to you, it's **exciting and intimidating** at the same time.

Section Two
measures your conscientiousness.

People who score higher on this section are often more **disciplined and goal-oriented;** those who score lower are often **spontaneous** and prefer to **improvise** rather than plan. There's societal pressure to be more conscientious – we want the people around us to take care of their chores and responsibilities (even if we aren't all that excited to take care of our own) – and many people can feel like they're hearing **"You need to take more responsibility!"** on an endless loop. But being too duty-bound can be restrictive, too – we probably all know the person who always takes on more than her fair share because she never says "no". As with everything else, it's a personal question of what level of conscientiousness is **appropriate** for the situation rather than one **"right"** way to be at all times.

Section Three

measures your extroversion/introversion; a high score means you're more **extroverted**, and a low score means you're more **introverted**. This isn't a test of how **friendly** you are – there are plenty of affable introverts and bad-mannered extroverts out there. Instead, it's a test of whether you draw **energy** from time alone or time with other people. If a party pumps you up and an afternoon by yourself feels boring, that's **extroversion**; if you like seeing friends or **going out** but need some **solitude** or time with a good book to refresh yourself afterwards, that's **introversion**. Some social groups and cultures are a better fit for introverts, and some are more comfortable for extroverts. The main thing here is to have a good sense of what you need so you can **manage your time** without getting worn out. Everyone needs to recharge, no matter how they like to do it.

Section Four

measures your "neuroticism". That's a harsh-sounding word with **gloomy Freudian overtones;** a better way to think of neuroticism is as a question of how easily upset you are. Some people are prone to **feeling anger, sadness, and anxiety** more frequently, while others take things pretty calmly. Having a low neuroticism score doesn't necessarily mean you're always **positive** and **happy-go-lucky;** it's just harder to rattle you. A high score doesn't necessarily mean you're an **unhappy person;** you're just more emotionally responsive to bad events. But if you also have a knack for getting over difficult feelings quickly, maybe a better word than **"neurotic"** is simply **"sensitive".** If you scored high on this one, don't worry (although you're more likely to!) – just think of it as a reason to try to be more aware of your emotions, and make sure you **keep an eye** on your own wellbeing.

Section Five

measures your agreeableness. Some of us are **cooperative types** who like to get along with other people, while some of us are more **suspicious,** preferring to make sure we're okay ourselves before putting ourselves out for others. A high score on this section means you're the agreeable type; **agreeable people** are more **friendly** and tend to get along well in a **team.** On the other hand, a **lower level** of agreeableness can mean **good leadership** skills; sometimes the group needs someone who'll push for the best result rather than worrying about whether it's polite to speak up. If you gave yourself a low score on this section, remember there are **positive** ways to be **"not agreeable"** without being **disagreeable;** some situations benefit from having a contrarian giving everyone a reality check, so don't let pressure to play nice silence your **real thoughts and feelings.**

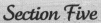

Your Ultimate
Playlist

Ever since we've been making tools, we've been making musical instruments: archaeologists have found animal bone flutes dating back more than 42,000 years! Today, in this technological wonderland where you can carry thousands of tunes in your pocket, you can't walk down the street without seeing somebody listening to their headphones. Whether it's a lullaby for a baby, an upbeat dance track, a victory chant, or the same sad song twenty times a day to help us get over a break-up, music is a special language in which we can tell ourselves who we truly are.

"Every **heart** sings a **song**"

Plato

♫ WHO, IN MUSIC, ARE YOU? CREATE A PLAYLIST OF THE **10** MOST MEANINGFUL OR IMPORTANT SONGS IN YOUR LIFE TO REPRESENT YOU.

1 Song:
Artist:

2 Song:
Artist:

3 Song:
Artist:

4 Song:
Artist:

5 Song:
Artist:

6 Song:
Artist:

7 Song:
Artist:

8 Song:
Artist:

9 Song:
Artist:

10 Song:
Artist:

♫ WRITE YOUR MUSIC MANTRA. WHAT DOES MUSIC MEAN TO YOU?

♫ LIST **5** PEOPLE IN YOUR LIFE AND A SONG TO RERPESENT EACH OF THEM.

1 Person:
Song:

2 Person:
Song:

3 Person:
Song:

4 Person:
Song:

5 Person:
Song:

♫ BONUS TRACK: WHAT SONG WAS NO. 1 THE DAY YOU WERE BORN?

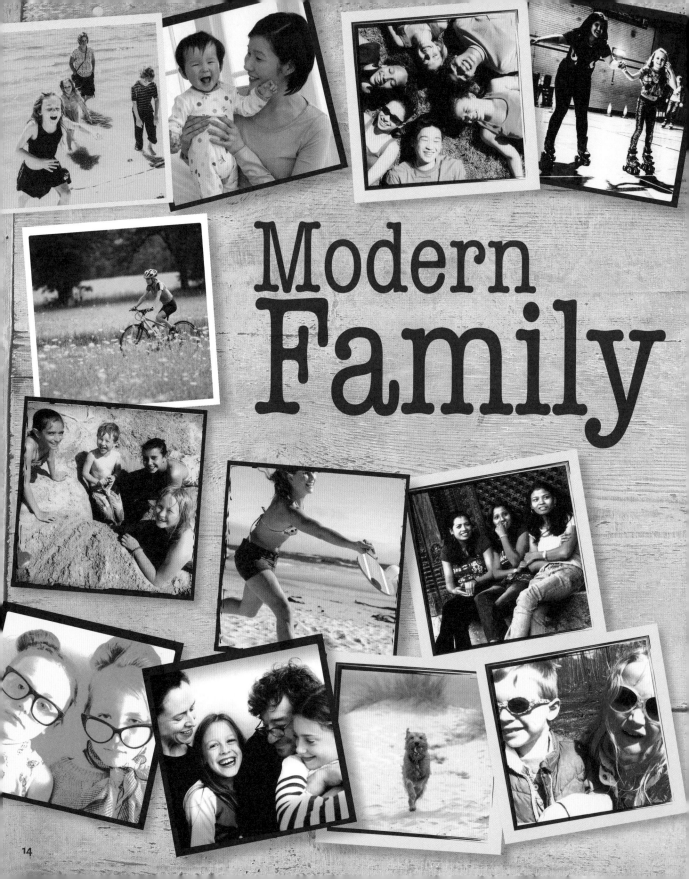

Modern Family

Family Matters

"Family" – everyone knows what it means, but if you ask ten different people to define it precisely, you'll probably get ten different answers. Family isn't who we are, but it is usually where we start. What's your family like and what does it mean to you?

1 WHAT ARE YOUR MAIN ROLES WITHIN YOUR FAMILY? ("Daughter and sister," "Grandson, nephew, and brother," "Daughter, stepdaughter, and stepsister," etc.)

2 DO YOU CONSIDER YOUR FAMILY MORE TRADITIONAL OR MORE UNCONVENTIONAL, AND WHY?

3 WHAT DO YOU LIKE TO DO TOGETHER AS A FAMILY?

4 WHAT VALUES WOULD YOU SAY ARE MOST IMPORTANT TO YOUR FAMILY?

5 HOW HAS YOUR RELATIONSHIP WITH YOUR FAMILY CHANGED SINCE YOU WERE YOUNGER?

6 IF YOU COULD SUM UP YOUR FAMILY IN A SINGLE MOTTO, WHAT WOULD IT BE?

Now turn the page...

Where do you fit in?

There have been studies on whether or not your family birth order affects your personality. It's an imperfect science; while most youngest children are outgoing, for instance, of course a youngest child could be introspective. Read the description that applies to you below, and decide whether or not it fits your personality.

ONLY CHILD

Only children experience less hierarchy within the family structure; without competition for attention, they can focus on their own needs and desires. Only children can be leaders and perfectionists. They tend to like independent work over being on a team.

ELDEST CHILD

Firstborns are often assertive and can be found in leadership roles, as they're okay with telling others what to do. Firstborns tend to feel responsible for other people, projects, or the world at large. They are dependable and respectful of authority.

MIDDLE CHILD

Middle siblings can feel "lost in the crowd" at home, which is why they're outgoing with friends. They are creative thinkers and can balance needs of multiple people at once. Often secretive, they tend to show their true selves only to their best buddies.

DO YOU FIT YOUR "TYPICAL" BIRTH-ORDER DESCRIPTION? Why or why not?

YOUNGEST CHILD

Youngest children tend to be outgoing and fun-loving, always looking for new adventures. They're comfortable saying what they're thinking and good at keeping a group's attention. Often spontaneous, they aren't planners – they're doers.

Your Family Tree

A family tree is an excellent visual way to keep your immediate family and ancestors straight. Each person in your family gets their own "leaf", and the lines between the leaves show the connections between people.

Use this page to draw your family tree. It can be as simple – names only – or as complicated – names, birth and death dates, country of birth, and so on – as you like.

WHICH ANIMAL ARE YOU?
Find the year in which you were born...

RAT
smart • wealthy • successful
sanguine • adaptable • popular
tidy • clever • personable
sensible • curious

PIG
gallant • calm • strong • tolerant
honest • frank • chivalrous
optimistic • quick-tempered • kind
light-hearted • generous

DOG
straightforward • faithful
courageous • dexterous • smart
warm-hearted • trustworthy
inspiring • stubborn • kind

COCKEREL
deep-thinking • honest • bright
communicative • ambitious
capable • warm-hearted
attractive • busy • neat

MONKEY
genius • lively • flexible
quick-witted • versatile • sporty
self-assured • sociable • innovative
practical • creative

GOAT
tender • polite • quiet • clever
kind-hearted • sensitive • faithful
wise • gentle • compassionate
cautious • circumspect

RAT
1984
1996

PIG
1983
1995
2008
2007

DOG
1982
1994
2006

COCKEREL
1981
1993
2005
2004
2003

MONKEY
1980
1992
1991

GOAT
1979

MY BIRTH YEAR IS ....

I AM A ....
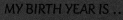

ZODIAC

OX
honest • industrious • patient
cautious • talented leader
strong-willed • contemplative
tender-hearted • amiable

TIGER
tolerant • staunch • valiant
respected • active • expressive
frank • honest • intelligent
faithful • virtuous

RABBIT
gentle • sensitive • compassionate
amiable • modest • merciful
romantic • interesting • soft-spoken
welcoming • comforting

DRAGON
lively • intellectual • energetic
excitable • perfectionist
ambitious • magnanimous
open • honourable • vivacious

SNAKE
good-tempered • communicative
gracious • moral • wise
independent • sympathetic
determined • intense • passionate

HORSE
ingenious • clever • kind
adventurous • talkative • perceptive
cheerful • talented • earthy • active
likeable • stubborn

OX
1985
1997
2009

TIGER
1986
1998
2010

RABBIT
1987
1999
2011

DRAGON
1988
2000
2012

SNAKE
1989
2001
2013

HORSE
1978
1990
2002

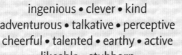

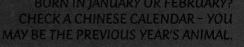

BORN IN JANUARY OR FEBRUARY?
CHECK A CHINESE CALENDAR – YOU
MAY BE THE PREVIOUS YEAR'S ANIMAL.

19

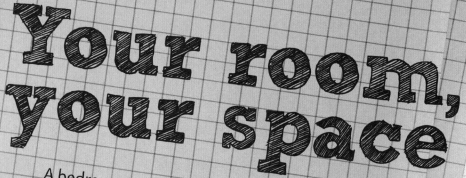

Your room, your space

A bedroom is a record of what we choose to keep, what we think we need, and what makes us feel at home. Look around your room. What does it say about you?

FENG SHUI

Feng shui – literally "wind water" – is an ancient Chinese art that seeks to bring people into harmony with the "qi", or energy, of the universe. The idea is that by arranging our physical space, we can direct the flow of qi in a healthy way. A bit of feng shui can make for a pleasant bedroom. This chart is called a "bagua map":

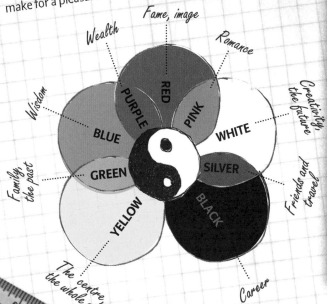

Use this space to sketch or redesign your room.

With your back to your bedroom door, hold the map so the red section points straight ahead. Then, devote your energy to the areas that you think need it most: clear away clutter, rearrange your furniture, or try adding a plant. For extra luck, add a colour that matches the element on the map.

True Colours

There are colours that look good on you, and colours you like to have around... but what colour is your personality? Pick one answer for each question below, then turn the page to find out.

1. TWO PEOPLE YOU REALLY CARE ABOUT ARE HAVING AN ARGUMENT. WHAT DO YOU DO?

A. Wade in: you'll always fight for whoever you think is right. ☐

B. Stay out of it: if you get involved, you'll just make things worse. ☐

C. Make peace: quietly explain each side's perspective to the other. ☐

D. Walk away: you trust them to resolve it, and you'll be there when they do. ☐

E. Distract them: suggest an activity you know they'll both enjoy. ☐

F. Let it go: it's not a big deal. Conflict's a part of life, and a good fight clears the air. ☐

2. WHAT'S YOUR PERFECT NIGHT OUT WITH FRIENDS?

A. Dancing all night at a great new club. ☐

B. Stargazing and a picnic in the park. ☐

C. Having a good meal at a quiet, cosy restaurant you all love. ☐

D. Hanging out and talking at someone's house. ☐

E. Catching a film by your favourite director. ☐

F. Singing your hearts out at karaoke night. ☐

3. WHAT'S YOUR FAVOURITE WAY TO GET YOURSELF CLEAN?

A. A quick power shower, water on full force. ☐

B. Anything with warm water and fresh soap. ☐

C. A soak in the bath with soothing music. ☐

D. A bath with bubbles and your favourite book. ☐

E. A long, productive shower – that's where you have your best ideas. ☐

F. A Jacuzzi with its jets bubbling and frothing. ☐

4. SCHOOL'S OUT FOR THE SUMMER. WHAT'S YOUR DREAM HOLIDAY?

A. Snowboarding on the slopes, or attacking a rocky trail on a mountain bike.

B. Walking through lush woodland, just you, your crush, and the singing birds.

C. Relaxing at an elegant spa, up to your neck in warm, bubbling water.

D. Lying on a warm beach with the sun, the surf, and a few good friends.

E. Following a fascinating, knowledgeable guide around the historic quarter of a cool city.

F. Attending a cultural festival, with life and excitement everywhere you turn.

6. YOU GET TO MAKE ANYTHING YOU WANT FOR DINNER. WHAT DO YOU PICK?

A. An exotic dish with lots of spices – something you've never made before.

B. A warm stew that'll give you a satisfying hit of vitamins and veggies.

C. Classic chicken, rice, and vegetables – easy, filling, and delicious.

D. Sticky, gooey, yummy macaroni cheese and an enormous hot fudge sundae.

E. Make-your-own tacos, with tons of fun fillings and hot sauces to experiment with.

F. A colourful salad with tasty nuts and berries hidden under every leaf.

5. YOU'RE BABY-SITTING A CHILD FOR AN HOUR. HOW DO YOU AMUSE THEM?

A. Arm yourselves with water pistols and chase each other around the house.

B. Get out the crayons and drawing paper, and work on a picture together.

C. Sit down with them and have a quiet chat about their day.

D. Build an enormous blanket castle, cuddle up, and sing songs together.

E. Pick out some books they love and settle down for a read-aloud session.

F. Find some of their stuffed animals and improvise a puppet show.

7. YOU'RE STUCK ALONE FOR THE EVENING. HOW DO YOU PASS THE TIME?

A. Plan something to surprise your friends when you see them tomorrow.

B. Get out your unfinished craft projects or try a new recipe for dinner.

C. Take advantage of the time to finish the homework that's due next week.

D. Put on your favourite film or TV show and curl up on the sofa.

E. Log on to your favourite website and catch up on what you've missed.

F. Blast your favourite songs while you lip-synch into a hairbrush.

Turn the page for the answers... >

True Colours
Answers

Look at your choices on the previous page, work out which letter you chose the most, then find your answer below. What colour is your personality?

MOSTLY A: Red
You're a bold soul with energy to spare. The world is a big, fun place for you, with new adventures to be had at every turn, and your enthusiasm and courage give a boost to your friends and family. Sometimes you rush in to new situations without thinking, but you always find a way to emerge with your head held high.

MOSTLY B: Green
You're a natural spirit, in search of balance and creativity. Peace appeals to you, but you like to keep your thoughts lively; people enjoy your imagination and open-mindedness. If someone annoys you, you can be a little impatient – but among good friends, you're a force of joy.

MOSTLY C: Blue
Yours is a tranquil light: your clarity and calm make everyone feel better. Life is something you handle with grace, and you keep a core of kindness no matter how ruffled things get. Under pressure you may silence yourself a bit too much, but you always know your own mind.

MOSTLY D: Yellow
You can make a home wherever you go, and your inner warmth draws others to you. It's in the people and places you love that you find your deepest meaning. When you get stressed out, you can find yourself stuck in a rut, but eventually you figure out how to keep yourself going.

MOSTLY E: Silver
Our minds were made for thinking, and you don't let yours stand idle. Curiosity animates you: even when you look quiet, inside your head there's always a new experience taking place. When anxious, you may have trouble sharing your feelings – but to those who really know you, you're endlessly fascinating.

MOSTLY F: Purple
Life is an adventure, and you don't intend to miss a single moment of the fun. Your quirkiness and sense of drama make you a treat to be around, and you can spot a good time quicker than anyone. Your strong feelings may sometimes get the better of you, but in the end, you can always find a way to see things from every angle.

" **THE PUREST** *and most* *thoughtful* MINDS *are those that* love COLOUR *the most.* "

John Ruskin, *The Stones of Venice*

WHAT'S YOUR SIGN?

Horoscopes are deeply woven into the fabric of our culture. Are you a stargazer or a sceptic? Check out your sign below. (Astrologers don't all agree on which dates to assign to different star signs – so we've used the most common ones here.)

ARIES The Ram • 21 March–19 April
Your element: **Fire** • Your ruling planet: **Mars**

Your strengths: Aries is an adventurer, full of optimism, and is always on the lookout for new opportunities. Other people are drawn to her enthusiasm, knowing that there's fun to be had around her. She's also independent: Aries is friendly and trusting, but doesn't need others to validate her.

Your weaknesses: Aries is not always patient. A frustrated Aries can be moody or demanding.

TAURUS The Bull • 20 April–20 May
Your element: **Earth** • Your ruling planet: **Venus**

Your strengths: Patient and steady, Taurus knows how to keep her head when the world's gone upside-down. Wonderfully loyal and brave, Taurus is reliable and full of stamina, a realist who can also appreciate the finer things in life. If you want it done right, ask a Taurus.

Your weaknesses: A Taurus can be stubborn, doesn't deal well with change, and is prone to being secretive.

GEMINI The Twins • 21 May–20 June
Your element: **Air** • Your ruling planet: **Mercury**

Your strengths: Ever adaptable, Gemini bubbles over with charm. Quick-witted and naturally expressive, she is flexible and tolerant with a lively imagination and a strong sense of independence. There's no one more interesting than a Gemini when she applies her intelligence.

Your weaknesses: Geminis can be fickle and irresponsible as their fast-changing feelings lead them astray.

CANCER The Crab • 21 June–22 July
Your element: **Water** • Your ruling planet: **The Moon**

Your strengths: Despite a tough shell, on the inside a Cancer is tender-hearted. Her feelings are deep and her loves are strong, making her a caring and responsive person to have around. Cancer is a nurturer, the kind of person people go to when they need a shoulder to cry on. Creative and forward-thinking, a Cancer stands by her principles as well as by the people she cares about.

Your weaknesses: If a Cancer doesn't keep her confidence up, she can get clingy and unreasonable.

LEO The Lion • 23 July–22 August
Your element: **Fire** • Your ruling planet: **The Sun**

Your strengths: Like the lion of her constellation, Leo is a ruler, with a glamour and presence everyone can feel. Leos are proud, and rightly so. Their integrity, ambition, and generosity make them true leaders. Leo has an independent soul, but she's not a loner; in groups, a Leo is the one people look up to, and that's how she thrives. Confident but realistic, Leo likes to keep things exciting. Underneath, she has a sensitive streak, but she always holds her own.

Your weaknesses: If her need for attention gets the better of her, a Leo can be melodramatic, domineering, and kind of a show-off. Leos need to make sure that they keep their egos under control.

VIRGO The Virgin • 23 August–22 September
Your element: **Earth** • Your ruling planet: **Mercury**

Your strengths: Virgos are analytical and clever, and they're naturally drawn to help others, putting their methodical minds to good use. Very little escapes a Virgo's observant eye, and you can bet that she'll put wrong things right. Humane and delicate, a Virgo works hard and is well informed, an indispensable member of the group with a natural ability to put people at ease.

Your weaknesses: Virgos don't always take criticism well. A Virgo can miss the bigger picture sometimes, especially if her worries are overwhelming her.

LIBRA • The Scales
23 September–22 October
Your element: **Air** • Your ruling planet: **Venus**

Your strengths: Intuitive and fair, Libra is all about balance and harmony. Her nature can give her a passion for justice, but she's also diplomatic and graceful in her dealings with people. Libras have the power to influence people without playing for personal power, a rare quality. They also have a love of beauty that extends not just to the physical world, but to what's good in humanity.

Your weaknesses: Libra has trouble making up her mind, and can seem hesitant or, worse, two-faced if there's a conflict.

SCORPIO • The Scorpion
23 October–21 November
Your element: **Water** • Your ruling planets: **Pluto, Mars**

Your strengths: Nobody has more willpower than a Scorpio. Intense, determined, and magnetic, she can pierce right to the heart of things, whether it's an intellectual problem or a conflict with other people. Scorpios are brave and passionate, prepared to do whatever it takes for the people or issues they care about, and shrewd enough to find a way in any situation.

Your weaknesses: A Scorpio's fierceness can get out of hand and make her aggressive. Scorpios make dangerous enemies.

SAGITTARIUS • The Archer
22 November–21 December
Your element: **Fire** • Your ruling planet: **Jupiter**

Your strengths: Funny, honest, and down-to-earth, Sagittarius goes at life with zeal. Sagittarius is an optimistic sign, with a spirit of enterprise and a sense of freedom that can be a breath of fresh air. They're generous and fearless, knowing that other people can't take away their strength, and they have a wild side that gives them an extra bit of zest and courage.

Your weaknesses: Sagittarius can be outspoken to the point of rudeness, not always thinking about the effect she has on others. Tact isn't her strongest point, and neither is patience; she's prone to overstep the mark and annoy people without meaning to.

CAPRICORN • The Goat
22 December–19 January
Your element: **Earth** • Your ruling planet: **Saturn**

Your strengths: Nothing stops a Capricorn's slow, steady rise to the top. The most practical and serious of the signs, she's all about doing it right, and her ambition is matched only by her practicality. She works hard and shows strong character no matter what the circumstances, with her patience and verve seeing her through the toughest of times.

Your weaknesses: Behind the sensible façade there's often a lot of insecurity. Capricorn can put herself under too much pressure and wind up cut off from other people, coming across as materialistic or aloof.

AQUARIUS • The Water Bearer
20 January–18 February
Your element: **Air** • Your ruling planets: **Uranus, Saturn**

Your strengths: Eccentric and imaginative, Aquarius comes across as either a rebel or a quiet dreamer; either way, she brings health and clarity to the community. She can be years ahead of her time, bringing her own unique perspective. Free-thinking, Aquarians see a world of possibilities.

Your weaknesses: Aquarius is prone to expecting too much of others, and commitment is against her individualistic nature.

PISCES • The Fish
19 February–20 March
Your element: **Water** • Your ruling planets: **Neptune, Jupiter**

Your strengths: Pisces is a tender-hearted dreamer who feels everything deeply. Filled with compassion, she adapts herself to the people around her and accepts them for who they truly are, giving her kindness and sharing her emotions freely. Often artistic, Pisceans know how to express themselves and can be profoundly inspired by the world around them.

Your weaknesses: Without some discipline or support, Pisces can drift into self-pity and become her own worst enemy. Over-sensitivity can be a problem, and she doesn't recover easily from the knocks life gives her.

Henna Art

Henna's most famous association now is the body art painted onto the hands and feet of brides – artists adorn the young woman with patterns that symbolize a long, happy marriage. But henna isn't exclusive to religious celebrations. Go to a music festival, beach, or park and you'll find plenty of secular, modern takes on the henna tattoo. Pretty, painless to apply, and you aren't stuck with it for life. What's not to love?

Whether for religious purposes or purely for fun, henna images hold a wealth of symbolism. Design your own symbols, or use this sampling of Indian Mehndi concepts to get started.

What henna designs do you feel represent you best? Draw them here.

Square
order, honesty, stability, protection

Heart
love

Flowers
joy

Pentagram
the five elements of fire, water, air, earth, and heavens

What is henna?

Henna is one of the oldest cosmetics in the world. It's a natural dye based on a plant which, when ground up and mixed with water, produces an orange-brown tinge that can leave a dramatic effect on skin.

Dragonfly
change, rebirth

Peacock
beauty

Paisley
luck, fertility

Scorpion
romance

Waves
passion

Eye
protects against bad luck

Circle
perfection, infinity

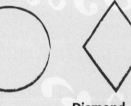

Diamond
enlightenment

These hands are shown palms-up to represent openness.

Triangle pointing up
masculinity, fire, ascent to heaven

Triangle pointing down
femininity, water, fertility, grace

Vines
perseverance, tenderness

Now You See Me...

Now you don't?

Do you show your real face to the world, or do you have a public image you're careful to maintain? Do you feel comfortable being your natural self around people, or do you feel pressure to fit into a mould that isn't really you-shaped? Knowing ourselves is a lifelong job but most of us have at least a sense of our own personality.

Give this activity a try. Here's how it works:

First, look at the words on the next page and **circle** the ten that you think best describe you as you really are.

Then, put a **star** next to the ten words you think your peers – friends, classmates, team mates – would use to describe you.

Finally, put a **tick** next to the ten words that you think the adults in your life – parents, relatives, teachers, coaches – would use to describe you.

What's the coolest thing you've seen or learned online?

....
....
....

What social media sites do you use? Why do you use them?

....
....
....

How is your online self different than your real-life self?

....
....
....

How do your e-friendships compare to your real-life ones?

....
....
....

Turn the page for more info... >

Your Digital Self

think about it...

Although the web can be fantastic, it's a double-edged sword – with every good thing comes a downside, and vice versa. Read the statements about the Internet below, and decide where you stand on each point.

Anyone can talk to anyone.

☑ **THE GOOD:** The Internet breaks down barriers and creates a truly equal space for people to connect.

☒ **THE NOT-SO-GOOD:** Internet predators. Need I say more?

I think that ....
....

Things can happen fast.

☑ **THE GOOD:** When it comes to organizing an event online, you can quickly move mountains.

☒ **THE NOT-SO-GOOD:** Incriminating photos or posts can go viral and get around the world in no time.

I think that ....
....

No one knows who you are.

☑ **THE GOOD:** Freedom. You can say what you really think or discuss things you wouldn't talk about with people you know.

☒ **THE NOT-SO-GOOD:** Haters. Anyone who's feeling nasty can be a scumbag anonymously.

I think that ....
....

It's easy.

☑ **THE GOOD:** Sending an e-card takes minutes, finding info for school projects is simple, and posting online gets a message out to everyone at once.

☒ **THE NOT-SO-GOOD:** It's easy to be nasty. A cyberbully can inflict a massive amount of pain, without accountability.

I think that ....
....

It's great for groups.

☑ **THE GOOD:** Campaigning for a cause or keeping in touch with everyone at once is a sinch.

☒ **THE NOT-SO-GOOD:** Vlogger Anita Sarkeesian calls it the "cyber-mob" – people ganging up on other people.

I think that ....
....

" **RARE** AS IS *true love,* **TRUE FRIENDSHIP** IS **RARER.** "

Jean de La Fontaine

new you RESOLUTIONS

Is it New Year's Day already? No? Oh, well. Never mind.

Resolutions we make just because 1 January is rolling around are usually the resolutions we break anyway. The ones we tend to keep are resolutions we make when we've found a new activity or way of living that we really want to stick with, or when we've decided that enough's enough and it's time to ditch a bad habit.

Think about it:

What have you felt most proud of doing recently? Have you tried anything new in the last few months that you really enjoyed? Or, on the other hand, do you have any bad habits that you're ready to break?

Here's a good place to start.

On the next page, create your "New You" resolutions: make a list of five things you've never done, and resolve to do each of them once. The good thing about small resolutions is that we're less likely to put them off because they aren't so daunting. When you try something new just one time, you win either way: if you try it and you don't like it, you still get to feel good about keeping your resolution. If you try it and you do like it, then you can do it again!

What are your five "New You" resolutions?

1
....
....
....
....
....

2
....
....
....
....
....

3
....
....
....
....
....

4
....
....
....
....
....
....
....

5
....
....
....
....

What's Your Number?

No, not your phone number. This is numerology, the ancient belief that the numbers that rule our mathematical universe also have a mystical significance. In this belief system, the numbers surrounding your birth can influence your whole life.

HERE'S HOW YOU ADD THEM UP:

Write down the numbers of your birthday and add all those numbers together. Keep adding the numbers together until you're down to a single digit between 1 and 9.

Here's an example for someone whose birthday is 25 December 2000:

(Day = 25)   (Month = 12)   (Year = 2000)

2 + 5 + 1 + 2 + 2 + 0 + 0 + 0 = 12

1 + 2 = ③

My number is:

I am the:

....

The hero

The good: Individuality, courage, a strong sense of self. Leadership and an adventurous spirit.

The not-so-good: Can be boastful, domineering, and impulsive.

The balancer

The good: Nurturing, considerate, and receptive. A sensitive spirit within, and a peacemaker between others.

The not-so-good: Can be negative, timid, or hesitant; may get overwhelmed easily.

The artist

The good: Creative, joyful, and inspiring. A great communicator and dynamic company.

The not-so-good: Can be scattered or unable to complete projects easily.

The maker

The good: Practical, clever, and steady-minded. Values order, and has the stamina to make things really happen.

The not-so-good: Can be stubborn or unimaginative and get stuck in habits.

The free thinker

The good: Self-sufficient, reflective, and smart; a charming scientist or philosopher.

The not-so-good: Can be too focused on perfection, sometimes to the point of meanness.

The explorer

The good: A fast-moving mind that crackles with insight. Versatile, active, and curious.

The not-so-good: Can be restless, discontented, and impatient.

The leader

The good: Powerful, with a good head on her shoulders, and willing to sacrifice for others; handles people like a pro.

The not-so-good: Can lack sympathy and push everyone, including herself, too hard.

The humanitarian

The good: Co-operative and reliable. Unselfish, with a sense of family and community.

The not-so-good: Can be bossy; doesn't always know when to leave well enough alone.

The open mind

The good: Subtle and compassionate; responsive to the needs of others and sensitive to the world around her.

The not-so-good: Can act irresponsibly and be fickle when new influences come along.

When you were YOUNG

When we wonder "Who am I?" usually we're thinking about who we are *right now*. Sometimes, though, it can be helpful to look back and think about who we *were* – whether we're still the same person deep inside, or whether life and choices have turned us into someone totally new.

Think back to when you were six years old, then answer the following questions.

What was your most valuable possession?

....

....

....

....

....

Who was your best friend? What did you like about him or her?

....

....

....

....

What games or activities did you play with friends?

....

....

....

....

....

Were there any people, places, or things you were scared of?

....

....

....

....

....

....

When you played pretend,
who or what did you pretend to be?

....

....

How did you feel about going to school
or doing school projects?

....

....

Were you a troublemaker
or did you like to follow the rules?

....

What did you most
like to wear?

....

....

....

Who was the most
important person in the
world to you?

....

....

....

If you could give your
younger self one piece of
advice, what would it be?

....

....

....

"" **I can't go back to yesterday because I was a**

different person then. ""

Lewis Carroll, Alice's Adventures in Wonderland

Turn the page to analyse your answers... >

WHAT COULD YOUR ANSWERS SHOW?

Were the answers to these questions on the tip of your tongue? Either you just have a fantastic memory or you're very in touch with your inner child. It's likely that you've kept a big part of the little kid who you were then as part of your personality now – and that you have friends, family, and photographs around to remind you of just how great that little girl was. Don't ever feel that you're "locked in" to the decisions you made and personality you had when you were a kid, though; if we let our six-year-old selves decide the course of our lives, we'd never grow and change. Allowing yourself to change can be difficult, but give yourself a little leeway and you might like the result.

Did you have a hard time recalling what you were like when you were younger? It's possible that you've let go of who you used to be in favour of who you want to become. Have you recently made a big change in how you choose to portray yourself, found a new group of friends, started a new activity, or joined a new club? These changes can take up a lot of mental and emotional capacity; no wonder thinking back isn't your activity of choice at the moment. That's okay, but keep in mind that our younger selves sometimes hold the key to who we really are; if you get lost along the way, looking back could be the answer.

Did you feel good while answering the questions? If answering these questions made you happy, that's great! We could all use a little more six-year-old simplicity in our lives, right? According to psychologist Jean Piaget, when we're six, we're more "egocentric" than we are when we're older – that is, we have a lot of trouble seeing things from other people's perspectives. It certainly makes the world simpler if we're only thinking about ourselves. Maybe you're feeling good reliving those memories because times aren't so simple now. If that's the case, let six-year-old you be your guide: what are your wants and needs in this situation? It's good to consider the wants and needs of others, too, but make sure you've got your own wellbeing in hand.

> **One can't get over the habit of being a little girl all at once.**
> L. M. Montgomery, *Anne of Avonlea*

"The most important thing when I was six was wearing pink – and only pink!"

Lauren, 14

"When I was six, the most important thing in the world to me was being a fairy princess."

Imogen, 15

Did you feel a little uncomfortable answering the questions? Are there memories in your past that you'd rather not think about? Or are you focusing all of your attention on yourself as you are now, rather than thinking about how you got there? Whatever the reason, thinking about your childhood isn't something you're interested in – you're at a moment in your life where the past simply isn't what matters most to you. Just because you aren't interested in the past now doesn't mean it won't come in handy in the future, however, so don't let those memories be lost for good. Consider writing down your thoughts in a journal or personal diary for safe keeping, in case you want to access them later.

"I loved my stuffed animal dog named Penelope so much. It is just as important to me now. It even went to college with me!"

Nicolette, 18

Is it difficult for you to see similarities between yourself now and yourself then? Has there been a big moment in your life that's changed you recently, or a realization that you wanted to make a big change? Or maybe the change has been quiet and steady, happening over time rather than all at once? Either way, who you are now and you were then may not seem at all the same. Try looking deeper: sure, you don't finger paint or ask to have the crusts cut off your sandwiches anymore (or, hey, maybe you do – no judgement here!). But when you get down to what's really important, what really makes you *you*, it's possible you'll find you have more in common with that little kid than you thought.

Looking back on your answers, do you see a lot of similarities between your younger self and yourself now? Are people who knew you when you were six always telling you how similar you are now to how you were then? Do you have a lot of the same likes and dislikes, the same talents and interests? You've got a strong core personality that nothing and no one can change. That doesn't mean you're overbearing or stubborn; it means that you're comfortable with who you are, and that all you've experienced along the way has served to reinforce that six-year-old's sense of self. You're nothing if not consistent!

"My uncle was the most important person to me when I was six. He's still important to me now."

Kay, 19

"I spent all my time collecting clothes and accessories for my doll. She was my best friend."

Jennifer, 13

beautiful world

There's a whole world of beauty out there, and lots of different ways of seeing it. Physical beauty might be the kind of beauty people tend to see first – but the truth is that there's so much more to beauty than just a person's looks. See if you can list five examples of each type of beauty listed here.

BEAUTIFUL POEMS, SONGS, FILMS, OR OTHER WORKS OF ART:

1

2

3

4

5

BEAUTIFUL PLACES YOU'VE VISITED OR WOULD LIKE TO GO:

1

2

3

4

5

BEAUTIFUL EXPRESSIONS YOU'VE SEEN ON A LOVED ONE'S FACE:

1
2
3
4
5

BEAUTIFUL SOUNDS YOU HEAR IN EVERYDAY LIFE:

1
2
3
4
5

BEAUTIFUL GESTURES OR DEEDS YOU'VE SEEN PEOPLE DO FOR OTHERS:

1
2
3
4
5

What's Your *Style Decade?*

Think you're out of style? Think again.

Some looks never go out of style – at least, not if they've got the right girl to rock them. Different decades made icons out of different kinds of faces, figures, and attitudes. If you've got the stuff that a particular decade built its look around, then retro may be calling your name! What decade diva are you?

Which of these words sounds best to you?

a. Chic

b. Classic

c. Feminine

d. Bohemian

e. Fabulous

f. Dynamic

g. Hip

How do you like your clothes to hang?

a. Sleek and simple

b. Crisp and tailored

c. Flouncy and full

d. Flowing and free

e. Tight and clinging

f. Big and boxy

g. Loose and relaxed

Which style icon below suits you best?

a. Coco Chanel

b. Ingrid Bergman

c. Grace Kelly

d. Janis Joplin

e. Donna Summer

f. Madonna

g. Courtney Love

What's your ideal hairstyle?

a. A sharp bob

b. A flattering up-do

c. Big, pretty curls

d. Long and loose

e. Feathered and fly-away

f. Sprayed and spectacular

g. Natural and low-maintenance

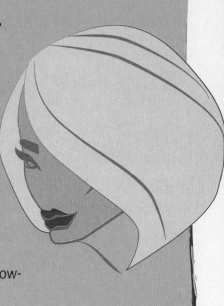

Which item sounds like the best buy?

a. A cute fitted hat

b. A tailored jacket

c. A bright print skirt

d. Flared jeans

e. A shiny, stretchy top

f. Colourful leggings

g. A T-shirt with a cool band logo

How do you like your make-up?

a. It's all about my big Bambi eyes

b. Minimal and neat

c. Big, heavy, and bright

d. Make-up? Not for me

e. Give me that cat-eyed look

f. My face is my canvas, all colours are welcome

g. Smoky and sultry

Turn the page for results... >

What's Your *Style Decade?*

ANSWERS

Do you have fifties flair or is flower power your thing? Find out your true style decade here.

Mostly Bs: Wartime Perfection

Smart and elegant, that's the ticket. For you, sharp tailoring with a military edge is what it's all about. This style is ladylike but also competent – the thirties and forties were when women proved they could go to work while the men were away. Your style whispers smarts and independence.

Film Fashion Inspiration:

Mildred Pierce (1945),
It Happened One Night (1934),
Brief Encounter (1945)

Mostly As: The Roaring Twenties

For you, it's flapper fun and freewheeling chic all the way. The twenties style is all about being feminine without being overly "girly". In its day, it was considered daringly androgynous, and girls who rock the twenties look today still have that air of independence and mischief about them. You're graceful, but you're not not a goody-two-shoes – and you know it.

Film Fashion Inspiration:

Love 'Em and Leave 'Em (1926),
It (the 1927 version, not Stephen King's),
Mad Love (1921)

Mostly Cs: Fifties Flair

With flounces and frivolity and a girlish swirl, you're sweet as sugar. The fifties were the great era of the teenager and a hyper-feminine style was in. Your style is all about enjoying your youth and prettiness to the full. You don't cut corners; you're going to look gorgeous and have a great time doing it.

Film Fashion Inspiration:

Rear Window (1954, gotta love Grace Kelly),
Gentlemen Prefer Blondes (1953),
How to Marry a Millionaire (1953)

Mostly Ds:
Flower Power

Peace and love, girl! The sixties and early seventies were all about the natural look, with a cross-cultural tinge and a fresh breath of freedom blowing. You're a one-girl festival, with a look that's artsy and colourful, full of imagination and dreams of what just might be possible.

Film Fashion Inspiration:
The Festival Express
(2003, set in the summer of 1970),
Hair (1979, set in the 1960s)

Mostly Es:
Disco Inferno

Flashy and fab, you're ready to burn up the dance floor. The disco look is all glitz and glamour, clothes that can catch the eye even through a dancing crowd. You're not afraid to be loud and lovely with a sense of humour to match. Go big, go bright, and go-go funky!

Film Fashion Inspiration:
Saturday Night Fever (1977),
Xanadu (1980)

Mostly Fs:
Material Girl

Bold and brash, in you the eighties live again. The eighties girl was scrappy and ambitious, with great colours and strong contrasts. The shape of her clothes – whether glass-ceiling-breaking shoulder pads or slashes and tatters – was equally powerful. You won't let anybody stop your rise to the top!

Film Fashion Inspiration:
Desperately Seeking Susan (1985),
Working Girl (1988),
Pretty Woman (1990)

Mostly Gs:
Gorgeous Grunge

Achingly cool and effortless, you're a wistful melody. Charity-shop finds are the prize for you. You long for peace of mind and have no time for primping when you can be timeless and authentic. You're a bit cynical about fashion, saving the drama for your thoughts and feelings.

Film Fashion Inspiration:
Singles (1992),
High Fidelity (2000),
Hackers (1995)

What's the Attraction?

Whether it's a romantic prospect or a potential new friend, we can find qualities in a person attractive for reasons that we don't always understand. The key to determining what makes people seem attractive is figuring out what's really important to you.

Think about the qualities many people find to be attractive.

How **IMPORTANT** are they to you?
How much do you **RESPECT** these qualities?
How often do these qualities help build a **LONGER-LASTING** relationship with you?

On the next page, rank the qualities in order of importance, from 1 (most important) through to 10 (least important), for each type of person in your life.

When finished, look at your rankings. Which qualities are consistently attractive to you?

IN YOUR BEST FRIEND:

Honesty

Kindness

Looks

Humour

Confidence

Intelligence

Style

Playfulness

Empathy

Creativity

IN A CRUSH:

Honesty

Kindness

Looks

Humour

Confidence

Intelligence

Style

Playfulness

Empathy

Creativity

IN A POTENTIAL NEW FRIEND:

Honesty

Kindness

Looks

Humour

Confidence

Intelligence

Style

Playfulness

Empathy

Creativity

IN A PARTNER ON A SCHOOL PROJECT:

Honesty

Kindness

Looks

Humour

Confidence

Intelligence

Style

Playfulness

Empathy

Creativity

Turn the page for more info... >

What's the attraction?
< How does attraction really work?

THERE ARE MANY DIFFERENT THEORIES ON HOW ATTRACTION WORKS. HERE ARE A FEW OF THE MOST POPULAR IDEAS. WHICH ONES HAVE YOU FOUND TO BE THE MOST TRUE FOR YOU?

Birds of a feather flock together

A popular theory, this phrase suggests that we're drawn to people who share our interests and opinions. The case for this theory is pretty straightforward; if you share the same interests and like doing the same things as someone, it makes sense that you'll have a good time together.

THAT FAMILIAR FEELING

This theory suggests that we're drawn to people who remind us of family members or people we already know. The obvious reason is because we instinctively feel comfortable with them. It can also be because we felt that the person we already know has let us down in some way, and we're secretly hoping to "make over" the relationship, getting it right this time.

> **" I always knew I would live life through with a song in my heart for you. "**
>
> Lorenz Hart, "With a Song in My Heart"

OPPOSITES ATTRACT

Are we drawn to people whose qualities counterbalance and complement our own? The case for this theory isn't hard to make, either: if you can cover for each other's blind spots, or make up for each other's weaknesses, you can make a strong team.

The role model

Sometimes we're drawn to people who have a quality we admire, and we feel we don't have enough of that quality ourselves. If the feeling is mutual – or, if both people see something in the other person that they really like – this type of attraction can be great. But it can also cause problems. When you first start a relationship with someone you think highly of, make sure you give yourself enough credit for your good qualities, too. Don't put yourself down because you think the other person is "better" than you.

The kind mirror

We may be drawn to people who see us the way we most want to be seen, because they allow us to be the self we most want to be. Like it or not, we all tend to change our behaviour somewhat depending on who we're with; if we enjoy a certain version of ourselves that comes out when we're with a particular person, that can be a powerful reason for wanting to be around that person more often.

Show me love

If you care about somebody, how do you show it? While love is pretty much a universal feeling, the ways in which we communicate it can vary a surprising amount. We can all think of that family where everyone's yelling at one another one minute, and are hugging and laughing the next – or that friend who teases you when the two of you are alone, but who will threaten to take down anyone who tries to cause you trouble. The kind of affection we're shown as we grow up shapes how we give and receive love, but we also have to find the style that fits with our own personality and comfort zone.

For each question, choose the TWO answers that sound like actions you'd most commonly take. Then, turn the page to find out what your answers could mean.

1
YOUR MUM'S HAD A ROUGH WEEK
and now she's feeling ill. Do you:

a. Pick or purchase a bunch of flowers to put in a vase next to her bed.

b. Sit on her bed and sympathize with the hard time she's having.

c. Volunteer to cook dinner and make sure everyone lets her rest.

d. Fluff her pillows and tuck her in to make sure she's cosy.

2

YOUR FRIEND HAS A BIG TEST
next week and she's nervous. Do you:

a. Take her out one night to do something fun and take her mind off things.

b. Let her talk out her stress and give her ideas on how to get ready.

c. Create study flash cards for her or ask if she wants you to quiz her on facts.

d. Give her a big hug and tell her not to worry, it's all going to be okay.

3

YOUR BEST FRIEND HAS LOST A CLOSE RELATIVE
and is grieving. Do you:

a. Help her get together old photos and keepsakes to remember the good times.

b. Listen to her supportively and share your memories of the person with her.

c. Offer to take notes for her at school so she can focus on family.

d. Let her cry on your shoulder and be ready with a hug when she needs one.

4

YOUR SISTER HAS BEEN OFFERED
the starring role in the school play!
Do you:

a. Buy her balloons and take her out to dinner to celebrate the good news.

b. Tell her sincerely that you're proud of her and can't wait to see the show.

c. Ask her if she wants you to help her learn her lines.

d. Grab her hands and jump up and down screaming in excitement.

5

IT'S VALENTINE'S DAY
and you've been dating someone for a few months. Do you:

a. Give roses, chocolates, and/or a present you know they'll like.

b. Choose this moment to tell them how you feel, maybe even to say "I love you".

c. Ask them to share their feelings about the relationship with you.

d. Surprise them at their front door with a kiss.

Now turn the page...

Show me love
How do you show your affection?

MOSTLY As: THE GIVER

Anyone can say "I love you", but it's in your acts and deeds that you give the words weight. Doing something for someone, whether it's giving a present or giving your time, is what truly means something to you. It's not necessarily about the money or things themselves; it's about giving your time and attention to another person and thinking about what will make them happy.

MOSTLY Bs: THE SPEAKER

For you, nothing should ever go without saying; it should get said, clearly and plainly, because if you care about a person, then why not tell them? You're a communicator and you want your love for someone to be like an open book – easily readable. It's words that are the window into your soul and you like to let them flow freely.

MOSTLY Cs: THE PROVIDER

Probably at this stage in your life you're not in a position to actually provide for people, but to you, love means making sure the other person is okay – because if you love someone, you care about their wellbeing. You want to be strong for your loved one and make sure they have everything they need; the best gift you can give is the feeling of being safe and secure.

MOSTLY Ds: THE HUGGER

Nothing says "I love you" like a warm embrace, a held hand, a pat on the back. For you, the physical comfort of a safe, kind touch is where love speaks loudest. This doesn't mean you're uncomfortable using words – in fact, if you can express yourself physically, you may be comfortable with expressing yourself in general. But for you, words alone aren't enough. You like to be affectionate with the people you care about.

"There is no remedy for love but to love more."

Henry David Thoreau

Super You!

Picture this: a cosmic ray hits you and (in an unlikely turn of events) you get to choose what superpower you want it to bestow. You have only five seconds to decide. Read the list of commonly desired powers below and go with your gut – which one leaps out at you first? When you've picked a power, look on the next page to find out more about your choice.

I can fly

I'm superstrong

I have X-ray vision

I can stretch in any direction

I can turn invisible

I'm indestructible

I have the powers of an animal

I can read minds

What does your chosen power mean, young hero? If you went with your first instinct, your choice may say something about where you are and what you need right now.

Flight

Are you longing for an adventure? Do you want life to be more thrilling than it is? Flight is the ultimate dream of being, literally, "above it all", of not being tethered to the ground by lots of responsibilities and expectations placed on us by others. If you chose flight as your power, you may have a sneaking desire for more freedom, excitement, and fun.

Strength

Strength is something we can only measure by testing ourselves against something, whether it's a heavy weight or another human being. The longing for strength is about our place in the community. Are you feeling under attack, or in a conflict you really want to win? Or, are there people you care about that you wish you could protect?

Stretching

If we could bend our way around obstacles, life would be so much easier! A wish to be stretchier means you want non-confrontational solutions to your problems – or that you'd like to avoid them without hurting anyone. If we could stretch, after all, we could get where we want without the risk of breaking.

X-ray vision

What's everybody hiding? X-ray vision wouldn't mean much if people showed us whatever we wanted to see. To wish for X-ray vision is to wish for the power to penetrate people's lives when you're not around. Is there a person in your life you suspect is keeping something from you, or doing something you wouldn't approve of?

Invisibility

Sometimes we get tired of having to keep up a public face; we long for the freedom to be ourselves without having to deal with other people's opinions and judgements. If you like the idea of being invisible, maybe there are places you wish you could go or things you wish you could do without having to fear the consequences.

Indestruct-ability

Wouldn't it be great if we could just shake off whatever life throws at us? If indestructability is the power you chose, ask yourself this: what is life throwing at you right now, or what risks are you thinking about taking? Do you have a fear to conquer or challenge to overcome? Being indestructible means having protection against possible failure.

Animal instincts

As humans, we have to be civilized – polite, nice, restrained. If we had the power of an animal, however, we could be physical, instinctual, free. Are you feeling trapped in your role as a friend, family member, or student? Are you looking to let out a little **roar** every now and then?

Telepathy

If we just knew what others thought of us, we could finally stop worrying about it. Like X-ray vision, telepathy allows you to find out what's really going on – but with telepathy, it's more about other people's secrets and private thoughts. Are you yearning for truth you think is being withheld, or for an honest connection with someone?

Relationships

Relationships are a wonderful part of life, but not even our best, most important relationships are a bed of roses all the time. In fact, most aren't. The truth is, a good relationship is hard work, with lots of ups and downs. It's up to you to decide if any particular relationship is worthy of your time and effort.

What makes a relationship last?

Whether a friendship or a romance, the answer's the same: relationships last when the positive outweighs the negative, and you can weather the hard times and still come out strong. Think about an important relationship in your life and answer the questions below to find out how you really feel about it.

You both want to hang out, but it turns out you want to do different things. How do you handle it?

a. You can usually compromise, but if not, an evening apart won't break you.

b. It's a pain, but you know there are plenty of other people in your life you could hang out with instead.

c. It tends to turn into an argument that's about more than what to do tonight.

d. If they're going to give you a headache about it, you'd rather do something alone.

e. You usually end up doing what the other person wants.

How do you feel after an argument or a fight with this person?

a. It took some work to fix, but it was worth it and now you can both move on.

b. You're never sure it was worth the fight; you're never going to agree anyway.

c. Still upset; you didn't really settle it very comfortably.

d. Annoyed; why did they have to create that situation in the first place?

e. Worried and frustrated, like you had to give up your own opinion for peace.

Do you ever consider ending your relationship?

a. Not really; you can't imagine any of your differences mattering more than what you have together.

b. Maybe; you can see reasons why you might end the relationship, but right now they don't bother you too much.

c. Yes, actually, and it worries you.

d. Yes; this person is bothering you more and more lately, and you're seriously thinking about calling it quits.

e. You can see why the other person might want to end the relationship, but not why you would.

How do you discuss touchy subjects?

a. You're both careful to hear the other one out and maybe make jokes to lighten the mood.

b. You both prefer to avoid them altogether when you can.

c. More and more often, it tends to turn into an argument when you try.

d. There are too many "touchy subjects" between you, and it's getting on your nerves.

e. You don't bring them up; you know you'll regret it if you do.

Do you tease each other?

a. You poke a little fun at each other sometimes, but it's always out of love.

b. Not too much, as it can put a strain on things.

c. Yes, though it sometimes turns nasty.

d. You do most of the teasing; sometimes it's the only way to say what you really think.

e. You tend to get all the teasing and sometimes it hurts your feelings.

What's the best thing about being with this person?

a. You know you can trust them, no matter what.

b. When things are going well, you have a lot of fun together.

c. You've had a lot of good times in the past and that means a lot to you.

d. They can be good company, despite their many faults.

e. You don't know what you would do without them.

Now turn the page... >

Relationships
continued

mostly
A

You're both onto a good thing and you know it. No relationship is perfect, but you don't expect perfection from each other; instead, you have loyalty and acceptance. If this is a romantic relationship, you're in a great place. If it's platonic, you may be looking at a lifelong friendship, the kind of person who feels like family after a while. Whatever your differences, you've worked out ways of managing them. Hold on tight: this could be a very important person in your life.

mostly
B

You might find that this relationship, while good, may not turn out to be the most major relationship in your life. You enjoy each other, though, and if you don't overload on expectation, this relationship could be a fun thing for the short term, or a nice, casual long-term relationship. Not every relationship has to be deep to be worthy. As long as you can focus on the good stuff, keep the bad from getting too big, and make sure you have other people in your life who can fulfill needs this relationship doesn't, it's good to keep this person around.

mostly
C

It sounds like this relationship, whatever it may have once been, is showing strain. Maybe you have a communication problem: when you aren't open with each other, minor misunderstandings can turn into major issues. If that's the case, you might need to work on dealing more directly with each other. It could also be that the two of you are growing in different directions. If that's happening, it doesn't mean you have to cut this person out of your life. Try letting yourselves drift apart a little and get some breathing space.

mostly
D

This person may want to be around you, but do you want to be around them? Sounds like you're growing tired of this relationship. If that's true, it doesn't mean you're a bad person. It can feel like we should be nice to everyone all the time, but sometimes we just don't enjoy being with someone. In the end, it's kinder to let the other person get some closure. End it gently, but do think about ending it – or at least setting some clear boundaries.

mostly
E

Relationships should make you feel good about yourself. It doesn't sound like you're getting that here. It may seem like you would be lost without this person, but the last thing you need is to be around someone who makes you feel bad. They may not be hurting you on purpose, but there's something wrong and the relationship isn't doing you any good. You have every right to end a relationship that you recognize as toxic or unhealthy for you. You deserve to feel happy and there are other people who can support you better.

Fighting Fair

One key to a good relationship is the ability to have a fight. If you know anyone long enough, sometimes conflict is impossible to avoid. But it needs to be a good fight, not a bad one. It should end with both of you feeling like the other person still cares about you, and preferably with your differences at least partly resolved. Here are some ground rules for surviving an argument.

DON'T

Call them hurtful names or say something just to make them feel bad. You'll only deter them from listening to anything else you say.

Bring up past fights. If you argue about everything they've ever done wrong, you'll never stop fighting.

Pretend to have feelings you don't. You won't get anywhere if you aren't honest. Own your ideas and emotions.

Try to get in last digs if things seem to be calming down. If you aren't satisfied, say so; otherwise, stay as constructive as possible.

Make threats or vow revenge.

Issue ultimatums that you aren't prepared to back up. That could land you in a sticky situation.

Throw things they've confessed to you, like a secret or a vulnerability, in their face now. You'll lose all of their trust.

DO

Consider keeping a diary to get in touch with your own feelings before entering into an argument.

Stick to talking specifically about what they're doing and how it makes you feel, not what kind of person they are.

Agree that, if things get too heated, you'll each say one sentence about what you feel, then let the other person take a turn. Keeping it simple keeps it manageable.

TRY THINKING OF SOMETHING THEY CAN DO TO FIX THE SITUATION, THEN LET THEM KNOW EXACTLY WHAT YOU WANT.

Concede any of their points you're willing to concede quickly and clearly. It's amazing how this lowers stress levels.

Remind them you care about them. Even "You're my best friend, but you're making me upset" can help.

Try empathizing with each other: take turns saying what you think the other one may be feeling. (Do NOT use this as an opportunity to get in more digs, though.)

YOUR 7 CHAKRAS

Are you feeling open and balanced today?

The chakra, meaning "wheel", is a concept sacred to many religions. Originally a religious concept, it's now been adopted by many as a way of visualizing and understanding how energy flows through us.

At various points in our bodies, we have a centre point where energy endlessly turns, like a whirlpool. If a chakra becomes blocked or out of balance, we feel uncomfortable or unwell and need to focus positive energy there to open it up or balance it out again.

Have a look at this chakra diagram and spend a little time reflecting. Are your chakras all feeling harmonious? Or do you think they could do with a little positive energy?

Blue
- Fifth or throat chakra
- Located: Throat, or Adam's apple for men
- Meaning: Thought, speech, communication

Yellow
- Third or solar plexus chakra
- Located: Solar plexus
- Meaning: Personal power, will, effort

Red
- Root or base chakra
- Located: Base of the spine
- Meaning: Connection to the earth, our fundamental, animal needs and nature

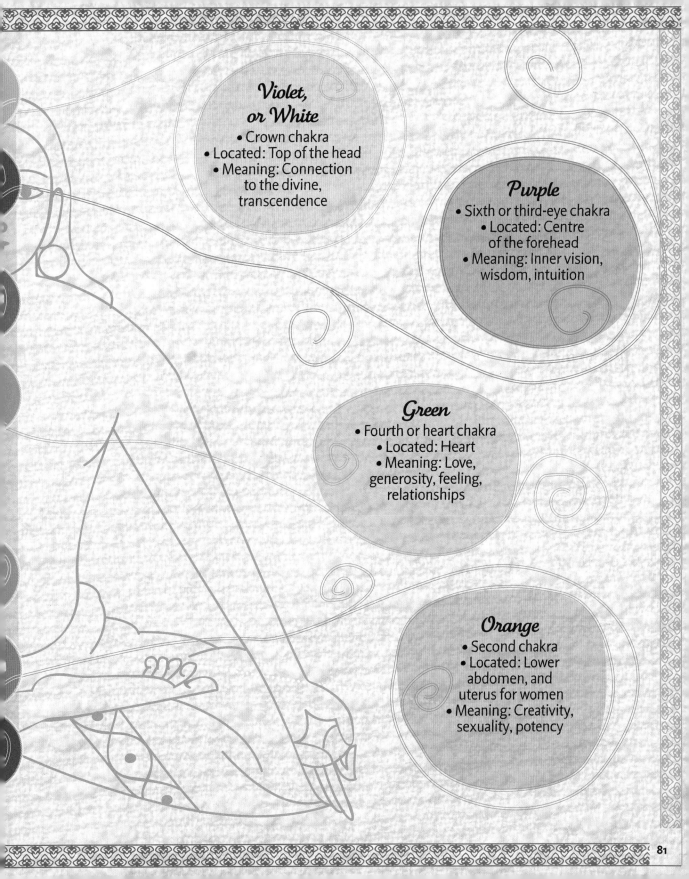

Violet, or White

- Crown chakra
- Located: Top of the head
- Meaning: Connection to the divine, transcendence

Purple

- Sixth or third-eye chakra
- Located: Centre of the forehead
- Meaning: Inner vision, wisdom, intuition

Green

- Fourth or heart chakra
- Located: Heart
- Meaning: Love, generosity, feeling, relationships

Orange

- Second chakra
- Located: Lower abdomen, and uterus for women
- Meaning: Creativity, sexuality, potency

Show me
YOUR PALM

It's an ancient art, perhaps as much as two or three milliennia old. Palmistry, also known as chiromancy, is thought to have originated in India and then spread through the world, taking on ideas from other regions and traditions over time. By the Renaissance, it was so well established that Henry VIII actually forbade it, considering it a kind of illicit magic that went along with sorcery and the summoning of spirits.

What do your hands say about you?

Well, to some extent it depends on who you ask: some people say that you can see someone's past in their left hand and their future in their right, or their private life in their left hand and their public life in their right. Others say that you should read a boy's right hand and a girl's left hand. Still others argue that you should read the left hand of a left-handed person and the right hand of a right-handed one. No matter what you believe, here are some palm-reading basics.

Heart line

If it's long...
you're romantic
If it's short...
you're independent
If it's deep...
you feel passions intensely
If it's shallow...
you're sensitive and flexible
If it's broken...
you may have love trouble
If it's forked...
you may have break-ups ahead
If you can't find one...
you can be ruthless

Head line

If it's long...
you're imaginative
If it's short...
you're practical
If it's deep...
you have a good memory
If it's shallow...
you can be forgetful
If it's broken...
you will make mistakes
If it's a double line...
you will be inspired
If you can't find one...
you can be lazy

Life line

If it's long...
you will have good health
If it's short...
you will have bumps on the road
If it's deep...
your life will flow easily
If it's shallow...
life may be stressful for you
If it's broken...
you will have difficulties to face
If it's forked...
you will face major decisions
If you can't find one...
you will be a worrier

The Girdle of Venus

If it's long...
you will be well liked
If it's short...
others may try to deceive you
If it's deep...
you have the skill to manipulate people
If it's shallow...
social skills may be hard for you
If it's broken...
you may be misunderstood
If it's forked...
be cautious with influence over others
If you can't find one...
you must make your own path in life

Destiny line

If it's long...
your life will be predictable
If it's short...
you must be strong in your convictions
If it's deep...
you may inherit good luck
If it's shallow...
some things will be disappointing
If it's broken...
you must be strong through hardships
If it's forked...
you will have conflicts
If you can't find one...
your fate may yet be undecided

The Bracelets

If you have several...
you will live long
If your bracelets are broken...
you will have illnesses to overcome
If they are shallow...
you must conserve your energy
If they are deep...
you are healthy and lucky

This or that

Tired of all that thinking this book is making you do? It's time to go with your gut. Would you rather...

circle the one that applies to you

EAT *delicious* ICE CREAM *or* SIT IN A *bubbling* HOT TUB?

HAVE A SPACESHIP NAMED AFTER YOU *or* A PUBLIC PARK?

BANG YOUR ELBOW *or* FALL INTO A MUDDY PUDDLE?

SING A NURSERY *rhyme* IN PUBLIC *or* WINK AT A COMPLETE STRANGER?

MAKE A HUGE PUBLIC SPEECH *or* SPEND A WEEK IN YOUR ROOM ALONE?

JUGGLE *flaming* TORCHES *or* JUGGLE CHAINSAWS?

GO OUT *dancing* *or* WATCH A MOVIE?

BUNGEE JUMP OFF A CLIFF or KISS A SLIMY FROG?

kiss SOMEONE YOU LIKE BUT AREN'T ATTRACTED TO or VICE versa?

RUN ACROSS A beach or ROLL DOWN A HILL?

EAT A LIVE CRICKET or GET SLAPPED IN THE FACE?

SLEEP ON A feather BED or WATER BED?

MEET A NEW person or READ A NEW book?

DESIGN A BRIDGE or PLANT A GARDEN?

dance or SWIM?

smell ROSEMARY or SMELL ROSES?

TAKE A TRAIN PAST beautiful VIEWS or SKI DOWN A MOUNTAIN?

Show Me the
Money

Whether you're a budding tycoon or aren't interested in your finances at all, there's no getting around it: money is one of those realities that we need to deal with. It's an uncomfortable subject for many people and most of us have a sneaking suspicion that we could handle our finances better than we do. It's useful to know what your general feelings are about money – especially if you're saving for university or a big purchase. There's no one right way to handle money, but it's never a bad idea to have at least a rough sense of your own strengths and weaknesses.

1. If you won the lottery, what would you do?

a. Buy yourself a huge house and a fast car right away.

b. Put the money in a savings account until you need it.

c. Put the money in a current account and enjoy the freedom to do whatever you want.

d. Hire a professional to manage your money and find ways to build on your newfound wealth.

2. If a family member wants to sit you down and talk about your spending habits, how do you feel?

a. A little guilty. Maybe you've gone a bit overboard on shopping.

b. Confident. You can reassure them that you're on top of things.

c. Uncomfortable, even if you don't have anything to hide.

d. Great! Maybe they'll have some suggestions for how you can manage things better.

3. You owe your friend a medium-sized amount of cash, and you can't pay it back when you expected. What do you do?

a. Ask her to wait. It'll come out all right in the end somehow. Probably.

b. Dip into your university fund or savings account to set things right.

c. Apologize and keep the subject on other things until you can fix it.

d. Find a way to earn some extra cash – you might even end up with profit if it goes well.

4. You've made a big purchase, way above your usual spending. How do you feel?

a. Anti-climactic and possibly worried; maybe you've really overstretched yourself this time.

b. Okay. You calculated it in advance and know you can take the hit.

c. Your nerves are pretty shaken, so you try not to think about it too much.

d. Pretty smart. You always make sure to get the best deal.

5. How often do you make impulse purchases?

a. More often than you make planned ones.

b. Almost never; if you have an impulse, you think about it for a while.

c. Sometimes, though you don't really keep track of them.

d. Only if you see a great bargain on something you know you'll need eventually anyway.

6. You're going on holiday. How much cash do you bring along?

a. Enough so you can get your shopping in – and your debit card, in case you need extra.

b. Exactly the amount you think you'll need for hotel, food, and necessities so you don't overspend.

c. You don't know; it varies so much from holiday to holiday.

d. Some cash, traveller's cheques, and promotional vouchers you researched beforehand.

Turn the page for results... >

Show Me the
Money
Results

Mostly As:
The Spender

Seize the day, that's your motto. Shop owners smile when you come in the door; they know a big spender when they see one. For you, money is about fun and freedom. Money isn't important in itself, but it's the path to a good time. Having a good time with your money can be great – as long as it's money you can actually spare. If you're wise, you'll stay away from credit cards, as there's nothing like mounting interest on a debt to take the fun out of life. Have you ever got yourself into trouble by overspending? If so, or if you're worried you might in the future, consider keeping some necessary fallback money locked up in a separate account. This way, you can keep enjoying yourself without those nagging worries spoiling the party.

Mostly Bs:
The Saver

A penny saved is a penny earned as far as you're concerned, and you want to be able to relax about the future by having a decent cushion of money to fall back on. Good for you; life throws things at us unexpectedly and some – okay, most – of those things have to be paid for. On the other hand, if you feel that it's never okay to treat yourself because you have to save every single penny, it might be worth reconsidering your approach. If you and your family are broke and saving is the only way up and out, that's one thing. But if you could afford the odd little luxury but never feel it's justified, remember that it's okay to reward yourself every now and then. Take some pride in your good sense, but don't punish yourself.

Mostly Cs:
The Averter

Money's a touchy subject and you'd really rather not get into it. There are pros and cons to this approach. You're much less likely to make money a point of conflict in relationships, for example, and that's a wise choice. Few things are better at creating pettiness and resentment than arguments over who spends what. On the other hand, you do need to look at your finances sometimes just to make sure they aren't going haywire. A good method for you is to have two separate systems: one account for unavoidable expenses that you can keep track of easily, and another for money you can use more whimsically. If you have a degree of safety at your core – the first account – your heart will be much lighter the rest of the time.

Take control of your cash.

It's never too early to develop awareness about your spending habits and to create healthy patterns. Building a structure around your finances now will help you meet your needs in the future. Whatever your habits are, you can work with them instead of allowing them to work against you.

Mostly Ds:
The Investor

Watch out, City slickers. You intend to make your money work for you. You know the value of money and what it takes to earn a pound. You might not be playing the stock market, or even want to, but you want to spend smart and save smart and make sure you always get the best out of what you have. If you can do this successfully, it'll be a great asset to you in life, as long as you don't let it come between you and your relationships with other people. The need to be a breadwinner can crowd out personal time, and sharp negotiations can leave other people feeling taken advantage of. If you can keep a strong sense of balance, you'll do well.

Where in the

Time to get packing!

If you could travel anywhere in the world, where would you go?

Which of these appeals to you?

A hot climate

A cold climate

Beautiful views

Lots of action

Exotic culture

Fine art and museums

Interesting local food

Extreme landscapes

A chance to "rough it"

Decadent luxury

Big cities

Beaches

People speaking your language

Spiritual significance

Great hiking

Charitable work to do

Scientific interest

Peaceful atmosphere

Grand mountains

Cool wildlife

Great diving

Extreme sports and activities

A party town

Lovely local music

Friendly people

A chance to unwind

world...

Make this map your own.

Mark places you've already been with a star, and circle the places you'd love to travel to someday:

Leader of the Pack

Whether you see yourself as a natural team captain or a key team player, try both questionnaires to learn more about your leadership and follower styles.

Leadership Quiz:

1. You've been assigned to head up a group for a class project. Your first move as group leader is:

a. Drawing up a timetable so everyone knows what needs to be done when.

b. Starting a focused discussion about the meaning of the project and what the ultimate goal should be.

c. Having a friendly chat and making sure everyone's comfortable with their assigned roles.

d. Proposing that you begin by working out how the group will make decisions going forwards.

2. You're planning a birthday party and your friends have volunteered to help. The first thing you'll do is:

a. Work out the venue and guest list, then assign your friends responsibilities to cover all the details.

b. Decide on a fun theme that will get everyone into the party spirit.

c. Ask your friends what roles they'd like to take on, so no one feels hurt or left out.

d. Come up with a few theme ideas, then ask your friends to vote on the best one.

3. Two of your friends are competing for the same prize. Your plan of action is to:

a. Equally help each of them towards winning the prize, but make sure they know that you support them both.

b. Talk over their bigger ambitions, so the friend who doesn't win the prize will still feel good about their future goals.

c. Be a sounding board for each, taking care to encourage them to stay friends no matter what.

d. Stay out of it and distract them with less tense activities when they're both around you.

4. Your closest friend has really let you down and you're angry about it. To cope, you'll most probably:

a. Make sure your other friends can be trusted to be there for you.

b. Question whether she really understands the principles of true friendship.

c. Let it go. You'd rather learn to depend on yourself than to lose a friend.

d. Sit her down for a serious discussion about why she did it and how you feel.

5. Walking home with your friends, you all witness a terrible car accident. Your first reaction is to:

a. Tell everyone to call home so your families know where you are while you wait for the police to come.

b. Think about the details of what you saw and attempt to figure out what might have caused the crash.

c. Check on the well-being of everyone in your group to make sure they're not overly upset or distressed.

d. Have everyone share what they saw so you can give one consistent statement to police or reporters looking for info.

Follower Quiz:

1. You and your friends are planning a trip and there are several different ideas proposed. Do you:

a. Generally stay quiet in the discussion and go with whatever most people want.

b. See if you can suggest some ideas that combine everyone's different tastes.

c. Put up some resistance to someone who you think is being too pushy.

d. Vote for whatever idea is the most different from what you would typically do.

2. You're on a sports team and someone's challenging the coach's way of doing things. Do you:

a. Stay out of it as much as possible; you'd rather not be part of the conflict.

b. Try to mediate or find a compromise between the two of them.

c. Keep at it, because it's probably you doing the challenging!

d. Watch the conflict from afar, taking in both sides and anticipating the outcome.

3. The bus you're on breaks down in the middle of nowhere and you and the other passengers – all strangers – have to deal with it. Do you:

a. See if anyone else has any good ideas before chiming in with your own.

b. Learn everyone's names to help you work together as you solve the problem.

c. Ask the bus driver to take charge, but make sure he listens to everyone's suggestions.

d. Ask everyone what you can do to be most helpful; you don't mind a good challenge.

4. A group leader is saying something you really don't agree with and she's not letting anyone get a word in. Do you:

a. Let it go. She'll talk herself out eventually and then you can change the subject.

b. When she takes a breath, tell her you see it differently but everyone's entitled to their opinion.

c. Jump in to tell her what you think; she has no right to dominate the conversation.

d. Sit back quietly and think about her words to decide if there's anything in them that might be worth considering.

5. You hear a rumour that your friends are planning a surprise party for you, but with a theme that you don't really like. Do you:

a. Drop a few hints, but if they aren't picked up, remind yourself it's the thought that counts.

b. Quietly take aside your most trustworthy friend and ask if she could help you out.

c. Tell them straight out that you've heard about the party and want a say in what's going on.

d. Wait and see what happens. If they think it'll be a fun theme, it's probably worth at least trying.

Now turn the page... >

93

Leadership Results:

Mostly A:
The Organizer

If it's got to be done, it's got to be done right, right? You believe that everyone has a better time when things are properly set up and everyone knows what to expect. You want everything to flow smoothly and for that people need to know their roles and live up to them. Under pressure you may be a bit of a sergeant major, so keep yourself in check if you find yourself issuing too many orders. If you can prove yourself reliable and sensible, people will trust you to take charge of things, knowing that with you at the helm, everything will turn out for the best.

Mostly B:
The Guru

You have wisdom and you're willing to share it. For you, the guiding principle of life is insight; you've come by your understanding and your sense of self through careful reflection and when you share that understanding, you can help show other people new paths to happiness. If you get carried away, you may be a bit of a know-it-all; never forget that other people's paths may be different from yours, but equally valuable. As long as you never stop learning from people, people will never stop learning from you.

Mostly C:
The Rock

You have a warmth and strength that people turn to the same way they might turn to a parent or a trusted adult, knowing that you'll handle their feelings with the same security that you'll handle the practical side of things. Don't forget you have your own needs – your friends can handle you saying "No, I need to look after myself" every now and then – but as long as you're as good at caring for yourself as you are at caring for others, it'll be hard for any situation to topple you.

Mostly D:
The Democrat

Your motto is: if it's not right for everyone, it's not right for anyone. For you, harmony is the most important thing and you move through your group like a diplomat – smoothing things over, moving negotiations along, taking responsibility for the right decision being reached. In your desire for agreement, you can sometimes pressure people to accept things they don't like or get overwhelmed by conflicting demands, but with good will from everyone, you're absolutely the right person to keep things fair and fun.

Follower Results:

Mostly A:
The Cooperator

As long as everyone's happy, you genuinely don't mind that much what the decision is. For you, it's being with people that's the main pleasure and you'd rather do your second-choice activity with a contented group than your first-choice with a dissatisfied group. Remember you have the right to your wishes being considered, the same as everyone else; as long as you don't dismiss your own wants and needs, you're a cheerful and relaxed spirit who can enjoy anything while in good company.

Mostly B:
The Peacemaker

Everyone's got their own perspective and you feel that the more people understand each other, the better everyone gets along. For you, it's about helping people see one another's point of view. Some things are out of your control, though, so don't panic and get caught in the middle if there's a fight you can't resolve. Keep your head and you're the perfect person to make sure decisions are reached based on a real understanding of where everyone's coming from.

Mostly C:
The Questioner

You don't mind someone else being in charge, but you do mind a dictator: a leader's got to be answerable to the group. You've got strong opinions and if you think a leader's making a wrong choice, you're willing to say so – maybe forcefully, maybe tactfully, but always openly. Be careful of needless nitpicking and power struggles, but that said, every group needs someone like you to keep things clear and keep the leader in check.

Mostly D:
The Learner

You're genuinely interested in hearing other people's ideas. Maybe they know something you don't and could expand your horizons. You're not particularly interested in being a leader because you learn more from trying someone else's way; you prefer to stay flexible and open to change. An open mind is never a bad thing to have, but don't forget to place value in your own opinions. Sometimes you probably do know best!

Come on, get happy!

What makes you happy – really, truly happy?
Happiness can come from a thousand different things,
whether it's a really huge success or just a tiny little moment.
Where do you find your happiness?

People who make you smile:

....

....

....

Places you feel at home:

....

....

....

Your favourite meal or snacks:

....

....

....

Activities and events you love:

....

....

....

Your most prized possessions:

....

....

....

Little things you do every day:

....

....

What's P.E.R.M.A.?

Psychologist Martin Seligman founded "positive psychology". He proposed that a happy life can be achieved through P.E.R.M.A.:

Positive emotions: feeling good
Engagement: getting absorbed in what you do
Relationships: having authentic connections with other people
Meaning: living a life that you feel is worthwhile
Achievements: getting a sense of accomplishment

Which aspects of P.E.R.M.A. do you have in your life? Which aspects do you want more of?

" I would always rather be HAPPY than dignified. "

Charlotte Brontë,
Jane Eyre

Get to work

"What do you want to be when you grow up?"

It's a question we're always asked, and a tricky one to answer. While some of us have an idea very early on and know where we're heading, others of us are far from sure. We may know what kinds of things we like to do, and we may even have some sense of what kind of person we are, but how does that translate into an actual career? Try this: **Read all of the following statements and tick those that you think apply to you.**

LOGIC

HELP

DETAILS

DEADLINES

1
- [ ] It's satisfying to put things in the right order.
- [ ] Meeting a deadline really pleases me.
- [ ] I rarely get stressed; I plan well, so there's no need.
- [ ] I'm not easily overwhelmed by lots of details.
- [ ] I can sort things out for you if you let me.

2
- [ ] People in distress often rely on me.
- [ ] I'm a kind person, but I have a thick skin, too.
- [ ] Helping other people out satisfies me.
- [ ] I'm not bothered by people who aren't grateful for a favour; knowing I did the right thing is its own reward.
- [ ] I'm good at putting people at ease.

RESPECT

INTERESTS

REWARDS

SKILLS

PROBLEM SOLVING

POTENTIAL

3
- ☐ I like working things out logically.
- ☐ I have the greatest respect for the facts.
- ☐ I'm naturally curious about how things work.
- ☐ I admire the great scientists and designers of the past.
- ☐ LEGO, chemistry sets, and mechanical toys were my favourites as a child.

4
- ☐ My imagination matters to me a lot.
- ☐ I like having time alone to do my own thing.
- ☐ I make and do things just because they're fun or beautiful.
- ☐ I'd call myself artistic.
- ☐ I like taking classes to develop my talents.

5
- ☐ I'm not self-centred, but I do like to show off a bit.
- ☐ Public speaking doesn't faze me.
- ☐ Stage fright can be an exciting rush for me.
- ☐ I love to entertain and impress people.
- ☐ Being the centre of attention is a lot of fun.

PATIENCE

6
- ☐ I can explain myself clearly and I like doing it.
- ☐ I enjoy blogging and joining online communities.
- ☐ If you want help with your homework, talk to me. I can help you out.
- ☐ I know how to deliver bad news kindly.
- ☐ People rarely misunderstand me.

7
- ☐ I don't mind getting my hands dirty.
- ☐ If you want it fixed, I can do it.
- ☐ Crafting and cooking are fun for me.
- ☐ When something in the house breaks, I know how to handle it.
- ☐ I enjoy feeling skilled and useful.

TALENT

ARTISTIC

Turn the page for results... >

Get to work
Results

The statements you marked on the previous page will give you a clue to the kinds of careers you might like. Count how many statements you ticked for each section, then read the analyses for the sections in which you ticked the most boxes.

1 EFFICIENCY
You find it rewarding to get things straightened out. Every workplace benefits from having efficient people around and some jobs, like working in a school administration, on a charity board, or for a company's management team, are all about efficiency. Being efficient is also a great transferable skill, giving you an advantage in any field you choose.

2 CARING
You might enjoy working with people in need and feeling like you're making a difference in the world. Caring is an advanced skill, requiring someone who can keep herself from getting overwhelmed by other people's needs without losing her kindness and sympathy. If that's a challenge you feel you can take on, the world needs you.

3 TECHNICAL/SCIENTIFIC
Anyone who works in the technical and scientific fields is the inheritor of a grand intellectual tradition – and maybe even a person who manages to push the boundaries of knowledge still further. It takes a mixture of curiosity and patience with an organized mind to succeed here, whether you're developing life-saving medicine or fun apps.

4 CREATIVE

All of us have our creative side, but for you, imagination and invention are a major part of your personality. A successful life means you get to live your talents to the fullest. While being an artist, actor, writer, or dancer are ways to go, there are also plenty of careers where these skills can be well employed in a team environment – consider book or web design, marketing, or architecture. Keep your eyes open for opportunities to explore.

5 PERFORMATIVE

"Performance" doesn't only mean getting on stage and doing a song-and-dance routine. (But it could mean that, too, if you're so inclined!) Many jobs involve performing: a professor delivering a lecture, a barrister arguing in court, a sales executive charming everybody at a conference... Look for careers that give you the opportunity to speak in public and sell your own personality, skills, and opinions as part of the package.

6 COMMUNICATION

While some of us like expressing ourselves in front of an audience, others prefer something low-key. If you like writing or talking in small groups, you're a communicator – someone with an instinct for explanation and teaching, whether it's in a school setting, in a business setting, or even in promoting your own venture.

7 HANDS-ON

You want to roll up your sleeves and build something. It feels great to do something practical and see the results. If you're a natural fixer or maker, there are many things you can do, from building something as big as a house to something as small as a computer chip. In this online age, people who can actually make stuff are increasingly rare, so put a high value on yourself!

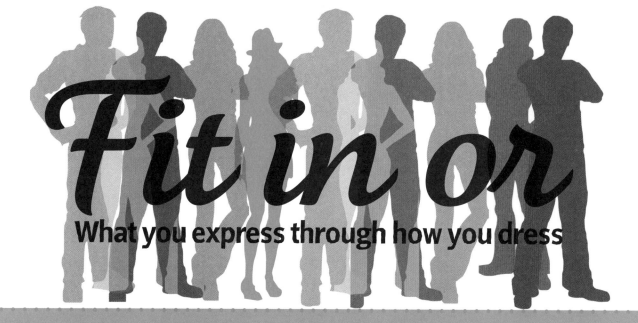

Fit in or

What you express through how you dress

We all have to choose something to wear every day, but what we choose and why we choose it can reveal a lot about the way we feel about ourselves and where we see ourselves in relation to others. Answer the following questions to explore your style psyche and understand what it says about you.

1 **WHAT PROPORTION** of your clothes are eye-catching, and what proportion are neutral and quiet?

3 **WHO ARE YOUR** top 5 style heroes?

2 **HOW MUCH DO YOU** change your style for different circumstances?

4 **DO YOU HAVE** a certain colour that's absolutely "you"? How do you feel when you wear it?

STAND OUT?

5 **IN YOUR IDEAL WORLD,** would what's in fashion change often, sometimes, rarely, or never?

....
....
....

6 **IF YOU HAD TO CHOOSE** between what "looks good" or what "feels comfortable", which would you pick?

....
....
....

7 **ARE THERE** particular brands or styles you go to regularly?

....
....
....
....

8 **WHEN YOU ARE BUYING** a new piece of clothing, what are the big factors you take into consideration?

....
....
....

9 **HOW OFTEN DO YOU** look at an outfit and think, *Ugh, why in the world did I even buy that?*

....
....
....

10 **DO YOU EVER SWAP** clothing with your friends?

....
....
....

Turn the page to analyse your answers... >

‹ What could your answers mean?

The Style Pioneer

Did your answers focus on your creative flair and individuality? Perhaps you're addicted to customising what you own. You're probably something of a trendsetter: you come up with your own ideas, and other people look at you and think, *Wow, I love her outfit. Maybe I should try something similar.* That can feel pretty good; everyone likes to have her gifts recognised. It can also make you pretty cool – as long as you don't use your powers for evil. (But let's assume you're way too nice to do that.)

Clothes can be a fantastic way to express yourself, and looking good often leads to feeling more confident about yourself, so you're definitely on to a good thing there. Sometimes if you're the trendsetter, it can feel like there are too many copycats around – but remember, even if people do seem to be trying things you feel are yours, it's your eye that created the look.

The Balanced Beauty

If your answers describe a stress-free approach – and an effortless sense of style – you're one balanced babe. How you dress is important to you, but so are many other things, right? In a stressful world, you're keeping both your looks and your head.

You're more about looking good than following the trends, and you're prepared to compromise when you have to. While you probably don't spend your nights dreaming of the catwalk, you've got a feel for fashion that gets you looking as good as you want to.

Dressing well is a skill, and you're at ease with that – but you don't let it rule your life.

> **❝ I express myself through my clothes. ❞**
> Kay, 19

The Social Styler

If your answers focused on how your style relates to other people in your life – be it your friends, your family, or your crushes – perhaps you're a Social Styler.

There are many non-verbal languages in the world, and you, my friend, are a fluent speaker of Clothes. Dress is part of how you communicate with people – your friends in particular. You use visual harmony to help create social harmony.

If your social group has underlying tension, fashion and clothes can become a symbolic point of competition. So if you seem to be having lots of friction with your friends over your wardrobe, it's probably a sign that something deeper is going on. If not, then hey, you're happy, your friends are happy, and there's always someone to compare notes with. Bonding with friends can make all the difference to your happiness, and clothes can be a fun way to do it.

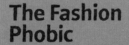

> ## " When I think I look good, I feel confident, and that's what actually makes me look good. "
> Lauren, 14

The Practical Girl

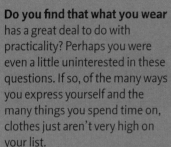

Do you find that what you wear has a great deal to do with practicality? Perhaps you were even a little uninterested in these questions. If so, of the many ways you express yourself and the many things you spend time on, clothes just aren't very high on your list.

You don't see your look as a major part of your identity. For you, clothes are a necessity rather than a hobby, and you expect people to be more interested in what's in your head than what's on your back or on your feet. If that's the way you feel, more power to you – just make sure you don't hold yourself back if you ever feel like trying something new!

> ## " My friends and I like to swap. It gives us more options. "
> Jennifer, 13

The Fashion Phobic

If you felt uncomfortable answering the questions, and find that you wear clothes to blend in rather than to express your personality, perhaps you're nervous about exploring your creative style. You know that people get judged on their appearance, and you know those judgements can be harsh. Deep down, maybe there's a part of you that fears you won't fare very well.

Clothes may be a big stress point for you because you don't appreciate or value how you look. Maybe you feel like there's no point trying to be fashionable because you're doomed to fail.

Well, here's a bit of news: when it comes to feeling nervous about your appearance, you're not alone – not even close. Six out of ten girls aren't comfortable with how they look. Odds are that the people around you who seem to have it all together aren't as comfortable as they seem. You're probably a lot better looking than you give yourself credit for.

The Repressed Style Icon

Do your answers hint at a secret style ambition? You may be secretly chic! A place like a school, a pretty intense atmosphere where people don't often choose to be together, might not feel like the safest environment to express all aspects of yourself – especially with something as emotional as appearance. But if there's a part of you that yearns to be a bit bolder with your wardrobe, don't write it off; fashion is an art form, and if you have a talent for it, that's something that should be cherished.

Keep your eyes open for any new opportunity to strut your own style, even if it's just for a party or special occasion every now and then.

> ## " I like comfort and prefer baggy clothing. "
> Mina, 17

ROSE
Love

Language of flowers

SNOWDROP
Hope

BUTTERCUP
Ingratitude or childishness

MARIGOLD
Grief

FOXGLOVE
Insincerity

BLUEBELL
Constancy

DAHLIA
Instability

TULIP
Fame

DAFFODIL
Regard

LAVENDER
Distrust

ANEMONE
Forsaken

CHAMOMILE
Energy in adversity

In the nineteenth century, sending someone flowers didn't necessarily mean that you loved them; instead, you could send a bouquet to warn, seduce, compliment, or even insult somebody. Floriography, the language of flowers, was a code in which a hidden message could be sent without a bystander getting wise to your real intent. Talk about flower power! Perfect for privacy, the language of flowers is definitely ready for a revival.

SEND YOURSELF A BOUQUET.
What **flowers** *best express your* **personality**?

DAISY
Innocence

CLOVER
Be mine

NOW DESIGN A BOUQUET FOR...

- *Your closest* **friend**
- *A* **family** *member*
- *Your secret* **crush**

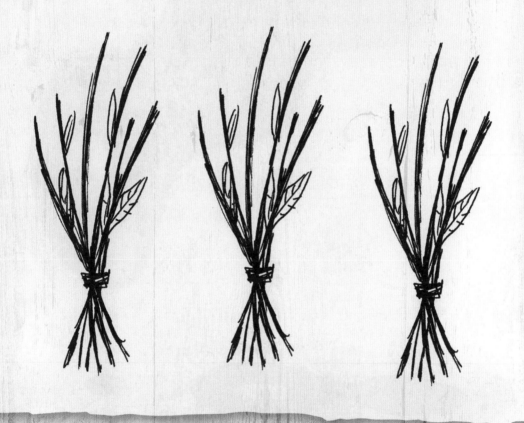

CLEMATIS
Mental
beauty

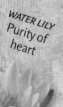

WATER LILY
Purity of
heart

ZINNIA
Thoughts of
absent friends

MAGNOLIA
Love of nature

SWEET WILLIAM
Gallantry

HELLEBORE
Scandal

HOLLY
Foresight

Fuelling Up

Knowing who you are includes knowing what foods your body needs to function at its best. Everyone knows humans need food to function – but did you know that certain foods can improve your performance at school and in sports, help you get over a heartbreak, or increase your chances of performing well in a test? Read the descriptions on the next page, and decide if you're fuelling up the way you want to.

Planning your plate

For specifics on how much of each type of food you should be consuming every day, check out the Eatwell Plate (www.nhs.uk/livewell/goodfood). The site has all the information you need to make good decisions about what you put in your body, plus sample menus and recipes, food safety advice, and more.

Obviously fresh fruits and vegetables are good for you,
but a surprising bonus is the benefit for your hair.
Add more fruits and veggies to your diet, and watch your hair shine.

If you're feeling anxious about an upcoming exam or audition,
don't overdo it on caffeine. Instead, keep hydrated and rely on small meals rich in lean protein.
If you have a sweet tooth, try eating a small amount of dark chocolate two or three times each week.
It can help improve blood flow to your brain, improving your ability to think.

Heartbreak can make even the strongest person feel weak, even nauseous.
Treat your broken heart with simple foods like
eggs, wholemeal toast, Greek yogurt, or pasta with fresh tomato sauce.

Iron is the key to avoiding fatigue and keeping your blood healthy.
If you find yourself feeling tired all of the time, consider upping your intake of foods like
lean beef, whole grains, and leafy greens. Nuts, eggs, and beans are all rich in iron, too.

Don't skimp on the calcium.
A deficiency now could lead to bone problems later on,
which you definitely want to avoid. Go with the basics, low-fat milk and cheese,
or treat yourself to some sweet frozen yogurt.

Planning a long career in a physically demanding field, like sports?
Get lots of antioxidants, which can keep you healthy as you get older.
Brightly coloured produce, like blueberries and peppers, are high in antioxidants.
The more colours you eat, the better.

If growing and maintaining strong muscles is your focus,
include lean protein in your diet in a big way.
Key sources are meat, fish, eggs, and low-fat dairy.
For vegetarians, beans, nuts, seeds, and tofu will do the trick.

Turn the page for more... >

Your favourite recipes

Now that you know what you need, use these pages to write your own recipes. They can be variations on recipes you found in a cookbook or online, secret family recipes, or your very own concoctions. (Banana-and-peanut-butter pizza, anyone?)

Recipe

Ingredients

Instructions

Recipe

Ingredients

Instructions

Recipe

Ingredients

Instructions

Do You Remember When...?

Some memories last a lifetime – shaping our sense of who we are, guiding our instincts and expectations when we look to the future, underpinning the story of our lives. At the same time, memory can be slippery. For instance, two people can have very different memories of the exact same moment. Sometimes we can even disagree with ourselves, remembering the same thing two different ways, forgetting something we know happened, or having a "memory" of something we're sure *didn't* actually happen.

Memory, in other words, really is the "story" of our lives. It's an ongoing story, mostly true, but also influenced by our personalities, imaginations, and relationships with other people. A powerful memory says as much about how we think as it does about what's happened to us.

What are your top five strongest memories, the ones that stick out in your mind the most?

1

....

....

....

2

....

....

....

3

....

....

....

4

....

....

....

5

....

....

....

Turn the page for more... >

Do You Remember When...?

ANALYSIS

Memory is a hotly debated science. Some people argue on the side of "recovered memories", or the idea that if something traumatic happens, we repress the memory and only find it again later through therapy. Others think that a "recovered memory" is actually a false memory, in which we essentially imagine something based on what the therapist was unwittingly hinting, and then remember our imagined event as if it were real. Likewise, there's a fierce discussion about how best to deal with upsetting memories; some psychologists believe that it's unhealthy to repress memories and that they'll pop up later and cause trouble if we do. Others argue that the unhealthy thing to do is to dwell on a bad memory, and that putting it aside is the best way to move on.

> **Many people believe that memory works like a recording device...**
> But decades of work and psychology has shown that this just isn't true. Our memories are constructive. They're reconstructive. Memory works a little bit more like a Wikipedia page: you can go in there and change it – but so can other people.
>
> *Elizabeth Loftus*

Happy memories are ones to cherish. But when a memory's upsetting, do you feel better working through it or do you distract yourself with happier thoughts?

Use this space to write about how you deal with the sad, embarrassing, or difficult memories in your life.

My friend circles

Friends I trust

Friends I love

116

Just like on social media networks, we put our social group into circles – those we love, those we trust, those we respect... Decide where in your circles you would place the important people in your life. Are there any people who fit into more than one circle? The overlaps can help you figure out what each friend truly means to you.

Friends I'd like to be closer with

Friends who inspire me

Tip: Add and label new circles in the extra space to make this page truly your own. (And if you're uncomfortable writing down your friends' real names, code names work just as well!)

What do you believe?

What would you say is your deepest belief?

How long have you believed in it?

What public things do you do for it – religious services, discussion groups, activism – and how central are they to your social life?

How important is it in your life?

How much of your time do you spend thinking and learning about it in private?

For some people, a belief or philosophy is the guiding star of their lives, the central truth on which all else rests. For others, their belief system may be part of them, but in an easy-going way. Still others prefer to take life as it comes, keeping an open mind their ultimate goal. Belief systems don't have to be religious – some people see science, veganism, feminism, or any number of other ideals as the centre of their values. Does something matter to you this much? Consider the questions below.

How important is it that your friends share or support your belief?

Are you close to people who don't share your belief? How do you navigate your differences?

Are traditions associated with it? Which ones mean most to you?

What, if anything, might make you reconsider your belief?

What do you like most about it?

Turn the page for more... >

< What do you believe?

This space is yours to write any other thoughts or questions you have about your beliefs.

"IF YOU ASK ME WHAT I CAME TO DO IN THIS WORLD,

I,

AN ARTIST,

WILL ANSWER YOU:

I AM HERE TO

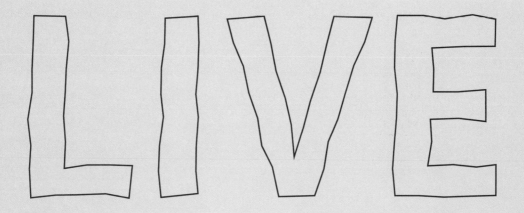

OUT LOUD."

ÉMILE ZOLA

For the Bookworms

1 WHAT'S THE BEST BOOK you've ever read? What do you love about it?

....

....

....

2 WHAT'S THE WORST BOOK you've read this year?

....

....

....

3 WHAT'S YOUR FAVOURITE BOOK? Were you surprised you liked it?

....

....

....

4 WHICH BOOK do you most wish you'd written?

....

....

....

5 WHICH CHARACTER from a book would you most like to be?

....

....

....

" *Ah, how* **good it is to be among people who are reading!** "

Rainer Maria Rilke

> " Everything's a story.
> You are a story –
>
> *I am a story.* "
>
> *Frances Hodgson Burnett*

6 **IF YOU COULD** meet one character from a book, who would you choose?

....

....

7 **WHICH BOOK** would you most like to live in?

....

....

....

8 **WHICH BOOK** would you least like to live in?

....

....

....

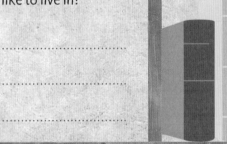

9 **WHICH BOOK** do you think everyone should read at least once?

....

....

10 **WHICH WRITER** do you most admire?

....

....

11 **IF YOU EVER WROTE** a book, what would it be about?

....

....

Decision time

How often do you hear people telling you to make up your mind?

For some of us, making a decision can be gruelling; faced with too many possible outcomes, we freeze like a deer in headlights. For others, decisions are made in an instant – but whether we stick to them or change our minds right away is another question. There are all kinds of decision-makers. Which are you? Think about the following questions.

1
How do you handle situations where you have to make a quick decision under pressure?

2
How often do you put off making decisions you're unsure about or feel stressed over?

3
Have you ever missed an opportunity because you couldn't make a decision?

4
Do you ever find yourself spending big amounts of energy making small decisions?

5
Have you ever let another person make a big decision for you?

6
How do you feel when people question the decisions that you've made?

Turn the page for more... >

< Decision making

Ever find yourself getting overwhelmed with all the different possibilities? Breaking down your options can help. This technique may help you get your facts straight before you commit to a choice.

STEP ONE:
Break down your options into a list, either mentally or written out.

STEP TWO:
Run each option through the following three tests:

1. What is the best-case outcome if I choose this option?

2. What's the worst-case outcome if I choose this option?

3. What's the most likely outcome if I choose this option?

STEP THREE:
Take your answers for tests 1, 2, and 3 and run them through *these* tests:

1. How will I feel if that happens?

2. A month from now, is there anything I'd regret?

3. What would I regret if that *didn't* happen?

STEP FOUR:
Compare all of the answers you get and use this clear info to help you make up your mind.

If you've got a decision on your plate, use the space below to give the breakdown technique a try. What other techniques do you use when making a decision?

....

....

....

....

....

....

....

....

....

....

....

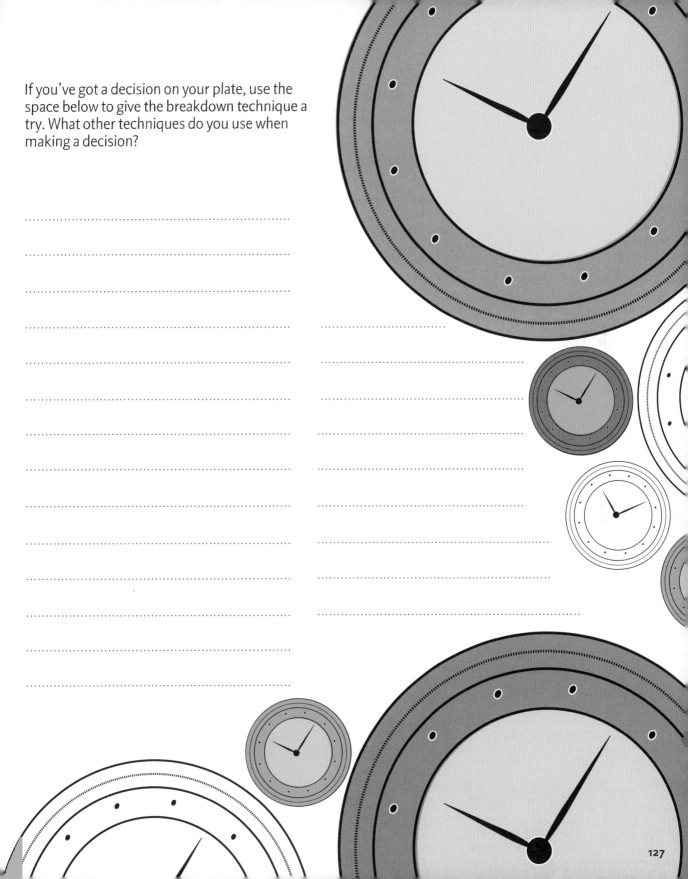

Keeping Your Head Straight

Weighed down by worry?

No one gets through life without worries, but it's possible to develop skills that keep your worrying to a minimum. One of the most effective techniques is known as "Cognitive Behavioural Therapy", in which people learn how to catch themselves in automatic thought patterns that magnify problems, then work to redirect them. The key is the **ten "cognitive distortions"** – ways we convince ourselves that things are more hopeless than they are. Taking the time to work out which of these you struggle with can help you on your way to a calmer, more worry-free mindset.

Which of these applies to you?

The 10 Cognitive Distortions

The 10 Cognitive Distortions	OFTEN	SOMETIMES	RARELY	NEVER
"ALL OR NOTHING" THINKING: You see yourself as a complete failure if you make a mistake, or someone else as incompetent or a total idiot if they do just one thing wrong.				
OVER-GENERALIZING: Rather than taking an event as just that – one event – you see it as part of a pattern of things going wrong, till your life looks like a long narrative of disaster.				
MENTAL FILTER: You pick out a single detail that upsets you and, paying far less attention to the neutral or good stuff, let that detail colour your view of everything.				
DISQUALIFYING THE POSITIVE: When you do something right or somebody says a nice thing about you, you dismiss it, deciding that it doesn't count or explaining it away.				
JUMPING TO CONCLUSIONS: *Mind reading* (assuming someone's thinking bad things about you) or *fortune telling* (convincing yourself something will go badly or wrong).				
MAGNIFYING AND MINIMIZING: When you magnify, you exaggerate the importance of a bad event. When you minimize, you shrink your good points and advantages.				
EMOTIONAL REASONING: If you feel it's true, it must be true, no matter the facts. If you're feeling bad, you and the world must really be awful.				
"SHOULD" STATEMENTS: *Should, must, ought...* You load yourself with demands and expectations and then punish yourself with guilt if you can't fulfill them.				
LABELLING AND MISLABELLING: You made a mistake? "I'm a loser." Someone annoys you? "He's a jerk." You use emotional language to make sweeping statements.				
PERSONALIZATION: Something bad happened? It must be your fault somehow – even if it really wasn't.				

The Power of Positive Thinking

If you're feeling upset or overstrained, try this exercise.

1. Come up with a sentence that expresses your pain or anxiety.

2. Assign a percentage to the sentence: Do you believe this statement to be 100% true? Or is it more like 95% or 60% true?

3. Ask yourself if you can find any of the ten cognitive distortions in your thinking.

4. Try to come up with some more positive explanations or attitudes for the situation. (Even if you don't entirely accept them, try them on for size.) While you're trying them, add up all the evidence you can find in their favour.

5. Assign a new percentage to your original statement. Has it dropped? (Bear in mind that it doesn't have to be down to zero: If you started out feeling "I'm ugly" to the tune of 90% and you're now feeling it at only 65%, that's still a pretty good improvement.)

This is one of those exercises that gets more effective the more you work at it, so try making a habit of it for a while and see how you feel a month from now.

In Love with Love

When you love someone, you try to understand their motivations and dreams. Maybe that's why we fall in love with fictional romances; as we empathize with characters, we practise using that part of ourselves that yearns for true love in real life. There are certain couples that people have fallen in love with again and again. Consider these famous fictional romances, and how you see yourself – or don't – in their stories.

Pride and Prejudice

It's practically become a template for the entire romance genre. Elizabeth Bennet, smart and funny but with no fortune and an embarrassing family, meets Mr Darcy, handsome, wealthy, and splendid. Their initial misunderstandings set everything on the wrong path: Darcy thinks the Bennets are silly gold-diggers, and Elizabeth thinks Darcy is arrogant and heartless. Can they reveal their true feelings for each other, or will their early mistakes ruin everything?

What appeals to you about this romance?

....

....

What doesn't appeal?

....

....

If you could give the characters advice, what would it be?

....

....

Romeo and Juliet

Young, romantic, and reckless, these two teenagers fall in love overnight – but with their families at war, they have to keep their relationship a secret. Tragedy intervenes and only after Romeo and Juliet die for love do the Capulets and Montagues mend their feud, too late for the poor young couple.

What appeals to you about this romance?

....

....

What doesn't appeal?

....

....

If you could give the characters advice, what would it be?

....

....

Casablanca

When they first were together in Paris, it looked like a perfect romance – idealistic Rick and brave Ilsa, clinging together as the Nazis destroyed everything around them. Then Ilsa disappeared, leaving Rick a cryptic note telling him she could never see him again. It's only when they meet again in Casablanca, years later, that each of them can rediscover their calling: to serve the world and stand against evil – even if they must love each other only as a memory.

What appeals to you about this romance?

....

....

What doesn't appeal?

....

....

If you could give the characters advice, what would it be?

....

....

Word Association

Your brain has to do countless things at once, from the basic "keep your heart pumping and don't forget to breathe" physical functions, to picking up the most subtle nuances from your environment and figuring out what to think and feel about them. With so much to balance, your thought processes can be pretty complicated.

The brain is designed to search high and low, go backwards and forwards, shuffling rapidly through possibilities in search of an answer. This is especially tricky when it comes to emotions. When there are so many possible answers to choose from – we can feel almost any emotion in response to almost any situation – it can get downright confusing.

How do we really feel? It's hard to know. This is where word association comes in. Psychologists designed the test on the principle that it's in first reactions, instinctive answers, that we're likely to find our true feelings.

This test is particularly good to do with a friend. Take turns being the "psychologist" and the "test subject". The psychologist reads each word out loud and the test subject answers immediately with the first word that comes into her head. See if you surprise yourself with what comes out! Use the blank squares to add your own words.

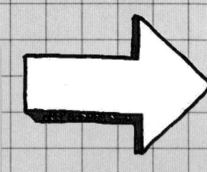

grow goals

sports

yes regret

dreams

change

Analysis

Thinking about your answers can be a good way of understanding who and where you are right now. Take the test again in another month or year, and odds are your answers will be different. But today, how do your answers feel to you? Have they turned up any worries you might need to address? Intuition is powerful and shouldn't be underestimated.

fun

loyalty

Pay Attention!

Do you ever have trouble focusing in class? Does your mind wander when you're talking to friends, watching a film, or trying to finish a project? Some people are able to target a single project, shut out the rest of the world, and get it done – but for others, focusing their attention on one thing at a time can feel like an impossible task. Answer these questions to get in touch with your personal focusing style.

1 Visualize a space where you feel the most productive. Where is it? What's going on around you?

2 What time of day do you tend to be the most alert? Is there a time of day when you find that you're least able to focus?

3 How often does your mind wander when you're in class? What kinds of things do you think about when your mind wanders?

4 Do you allow yourself breaks when you're having a hard time focusing on or finishing a project?

5 Do you ever put off tasks you don't want to do? If so, what kinds of tasks do you put off?

....

....

....

....

6 How do you decide which projects or homework assignments you're going to focus on first?

....

....

....

....

....

Turn the page for more... >

Pay Attention!
analysis

What could your answers show?

1

When you visualized your most productive space, was it a quiet room or a bustling public space? Some people crave a calm environment, while others think working in a lively atmosphere inspires them. Knowing what kind of place best helps you concentrate and setting your stage with helpful props – a mug of tea or coffee, your favourite pen, a certain song on your iPod – can help you find your focused zone.

2

Do you wake up refreshed and ready to seize your day and the challenges ahead? Or do you think best when you're burning the midnight oil? Honouring your internal rhythm can help you work out when you're best able to achieve good concentration. Of course, there are times when you have to get yourself focused, no matter what your internal clock says. For these times, make sure you're as well rested and well fed as possible; body and brain chemistry play an important role in your ability to focus.

3

If you find your mind wandering, or if you get only halfway through one idea or project before your mind leaps to the next, consider taking active steps to direct your awareness back where you need it. Tell yourself not to start something new until you've finished what you're working on. You might also want to try meditation, which can help you attune to one subject at a time and clear your mind of unwanted thoughts or distracting chatter.

4

Taking a break when you need it is a great idea. Get up and go for a walk, or let yourself go online, but only for a limited time. It's key you stick to the rules you set for yourself or you could find yourself completely derailed from the project at hand. Give yourself a short study break reward, and return to your task with a fresh mind.

5

Putting something off is called "avoidance", and when we're dreading a task, we all do it. Usually, though, avoidance is just spending extra time worrying. The stress doesn't go away, and it's likely to prevent us from enjoying whatever we're doing to procrastinate. Once you actually settle down to doing what you need to do, the job will come into focus as a specific problem to fix rather than an all-encompassing anxiety, and you can start getting it under control. Put yourself out of your misery!

6

Prioritize, prioritize, prioritize! Putting things in order and taking things one step at a time will help you get the job done, and they will also help you to not get overwhelmed. It's much easier to focus on the smaller chunks of any larger project; putting those smaller chunks in order is the first step to knocking a big task off your to-do list.

"**Imagination**
IS THE ONLY KEY
TO THE FUTURE.
Without it
NONE EXISTS –
With it
ALL THINGS ARE
POSSIBLE."

Ida Tarbell

What do you doodle?

We're not supposed to do it, but often our pens get the better of us and we end up drawing doodles in the margins of whatever we're supposed to be working on. Do you ever wonder if your doodles actually mean anything? Doodle around on this page or look through the doodles in your notebooks, then see if any of the analysis rings a bell.

Straight, angular lines: you may be struggling to organize your thoughts or keep focused.

Curved lines: you're feeling relaxed and open.

Attractive faces: you're feeling friendly or aspirational.

Ugly faces: you may be feeling defensive or silly.

Trees represent life or vitality. (Is your tree healthy or sickly?)

Colouring in shapes is indicative of boredom, a sense of "filling in" time.

Flowers are associated with love and the soul. (Are your flowers blooming freely or are they struggling?)

Leaves or feathers: natural and almost symmetrical, these suggest wanting a sense of balance.

Animals are stand-ins for your spirit. (What sort of moods are your animals in?)

What types of images do you find yourself doodling again and again? What do they represent to you?

Monsters: if grotesque, you may be finding a person or situation monstrous – or you might have a wild side you don't get to express in ordinary life.

Cars are representative of freedom and power.

Machines are suggestive of intricacy and analysis. *(Are you looking for an intellectual challenge?)*

Weapons imply unexpressed aggression or a desire for power or excellence.

Buildings evoke a desire for a home – not necessarily your own house, but a comfortable mental or social space.

Enneagram Personalities

The enneagram test, developed in the 1970s, is popular in business management and spirituality groups. It's based on the concept of nine different basic personality types, one of which will be your "core" personality type. You can also have "wings" to your personality, which is where you share some traits with a type that's next to you on the circle. For example, you could be a core One with a Two wing, or you could be a core One with a Nine wing.

Each core personality type can have a healthy or an unhealthy way of expressing itself; therefore, two people who have the same personality type can, in real life, have totally different life paths. According to the enneagram, there's no one right way to be; instead, the idea is to be the healthiest version of your natural self.

Read over the personality types on the next few pages. Which sounds most like you? That's your core type. Do you have a personality wing, too?

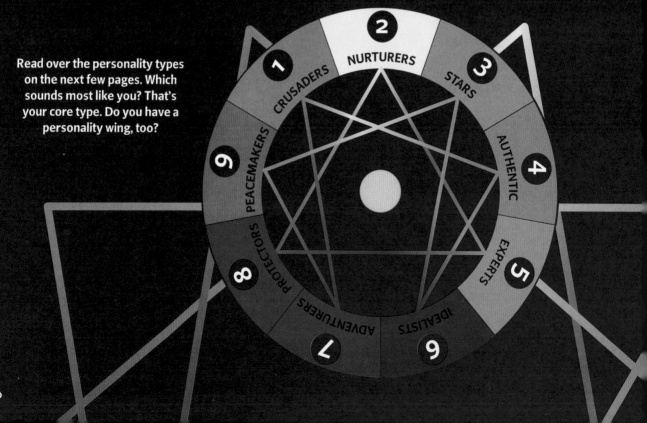

**ONES
ARE CRUSADERS,**
whether for a public cause or for a
personal ideal. Their ultimate goal is
to live a justified life. While they may
come across as rational on the surface,
deep down it's emotion that comes first,
and they find ways to make the "logic"
work later. At their best, Ones are
objective but passionate, the kind of
person who can really change
the world. At their worst, Ones
can be self-righteous and
judgemental.

**TWOS
ARE NURTURERS.**
They want very much to be loved
and they feel that the best way to make
this happen is to do things for other
people. While they may appear strong, they
are often secretly struggling with a desire to
be appreciated. At their best, Twos accept
their own needs while remaining warmly
connected to others, the lively centre of a
circle of mutual kindness. When
unhealthy, Twos can grow angry and
controlling towards those they
see as ungrateful.

**THREES
ARE THE STARS OF
THE WORLD.**
They want to develop themselves
and be seen doing well. Confident on
the surface, there's often a lot more
vulnerability behind the golden mask than
they're comfortable letting other people see.
At their healthiest, Threes are natural
teachers and mentors; they see talents of
other people and feel that other people's
successes will only enhance their own.
Unhealthy, they can be competitive
and cruel, or show off rather
than be honest.

Turn the page for more... >

< Enneagram Personalities

FIVES ARE NATURAL EXPERTS.

Whatever they do, they want to do right, and they'll go to any lengths to advance their skills and knowledge in their chosen fields. To understand things so they can master them is their real goal. By nature introverted and unconventional, unhealthy Fives can cut themselves off from reality and become isolated. When healthy, Fives are independent and original, breaking new ground and advancing everyone's understanding.

EXPERTS

5

FOURS ARE ALL ABOUT AUTHENTICITY.

Feeling somehow different from everyone else, they want to be sure that they're being their real selves. That sense of difference can have a light or a dark side. At their worst, Fours can feel melancholy, sure that everyone will misjudge them. But at their best, Fours can learn from their own strong feelings and find insight and compassion for the universal feelings of humanity, becoming honest, expressive, and genuinely unique.

AUTHENTIC

4

SIXES ARE THE CYNICAL IDEALISTS.

They believe it's a rough world out there and they're suspicious of most people. But if they can find a person to admire or a cause to serve, nothing breaks their loyalty. Under that wry façade is an anxious person who wants to do right and feels they need support to do so. When unhealthy, Sixes can be authoritarian and paranoid, blaming scapegoats, but when healthy, they are dependable and loving, an indispensable force for good.

IDEALISTS

6

SEVENS ARE ADVENTURERS

who want to try everything life has to offer. For a Seven, anticipation is always a thrill and the future is filled with possibilities. Healthy Sevens are generous and delightful, channelling their energy in positive directions and becoming funny and fun, making themselves and everyone around them happy. When unhealthy, Sevens can be abrasive and callous in their pursuit of gratification, and impatient with anyone who won't do things the way they want to.

ADVENTURERS

7

EIGHTS ARE PROTECTORS,

both of themselves and other people. Practical, strong, and unafraid of a confrontation, an Eight is the first person you want on your side in a conflict, but the last person you want against you, as an unhealthy Eight can be vengeful, bullying, and merciless. When healthy, though, an Eight is the rock that everyone can rely on. Eights find peace by connecting to their simple desire to do right by everyone, and to be loved and trusted by the people they care about the most.

PROTECTORS

8

NINES ARE PEACEMAKERS,

but don't let that fool you into thinking they're weak. What Nines want most is to be connected and at ease; they have a lot of strength to them, but they direct it towards avoiding conflict and seeking harmony. Nines who accept their own strengths are peaceful and honest, often with a playful sense of humour and a deep appreciation for happiness. When unhealthy, Nines can be stubborn and passive-aggressive, choosing to see only the things they want to see.

PEACEMAKERS

9

1 2 3 9 6 4 8 5 7 9

I think my core personality is:

I think my wing personality is:

Calling All Daredevils

⚠️
GROUP 2

- Sneaking into an 18-rated film
- Flirting with someone forbidden
- Getting away with a lie
- Wearing outfits your family doesn't approve of
- Passing a note in class
- Talking back to teachers
- Spraying graffiti
- Talking to people your friends think are trouble
- Going out when you're supposed to be grounded
- Bunking off a job or sports practice early

⚠️
GROUP 3

- Staring down a creepy stranger
- Saying to a friend, "Yes, your bum does look big in that"
- Sharing secrets that aren't yours
- Telling one of your classmates exactly how offensive they're being
- Going all-out in a debate
- Telling a relative just how weird he really is
- Telling a telemarketer it's rude to bother people
- Telling someone their joke wasn't funny

⚠️
GROUP 1

- Paintballing
- Riding a roller coaster
- Skiing
- Driving a racing car
- Skydiving
- Roller derby
- Boxing or wrestling
- Riding a motorcycle
- Jet skiing
- Rock climbing

When it comes to taking risks, how far would you go? Tick the box next to the activities you've either done or would do if you could, then turn the page.

GROUP 4

- Entering a competition
- Telling a crush how you feel
- Making a bet
- Applying for a long-shot apprenticeship or sports team
- Writing a poem or letter and sending it in to a lit mag
- Giving someone an ultimatum
- Making a pact with a friend to give something up if she does
- Playing a game when money's at stake
- Learning a new craft skill to make a gift for someone
- Going on a blind date

GROUP 5

- Watching a horror movie
- Planning out a big argument with someone
- Watching a viral video about someone overcoming tragedy
- Watching the televised funeral of a major public figure
- Letting a close friend tell you an emotional secret
- Attending a lecture given by a disaster survivor
- Listening to a song that makes you cry
- Following a political scandal
- Looking for big gossip about your favourite celebrity
- Reading a true-crime book

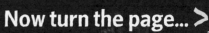

Now turn the page... >

Calling All Daredevils
analysis

Each group tests a different kind of daring.
Count how many statements you ticked
in each group, then read on to learn more.

GROUP 1 — Relishing the Rush

Five or more: Hello, adrenaline junkie! There's nothing like a good rush to make you feel alive. Physical challenges can be some of the greatest moments you'll ever experience. You may not actually put yourself in danger – there are all sorts of pretty safe sports, games, and experiences that allow you to feel the thrill of risk without putting your life on the line. (And that's good news for people like you!) As long as you keep it sensible and safe, your life will be a lot of fun.

Four or fewer: Were you thinking, "Um, no way", when you read these activities? The kind of high-impact stimulation that you get from extreme sports is more than you want or need. Leave the bungee jumping, skydiving, and rock climbing to those who enjoy it!

GROUP 2 — Breaking the Rules

Six or more: You're attracted to defying societal convention. Society enforces its norms – and some are there for good reason. Others, though, may seem pointless to you, and you like to push the boundaries.

Three to five: You're more the conscientious type. You know the rules and you stick to them. Just make sure you understand why a rule's in place before you follow it; unwise people can make rules, too.

Two or fewer: Did you look at the list and think, "No way, I couldn't stand the tension?" You may have a fear of disapproval. If you're just worried about upsetting people, that's an active conscience at work. But if the idea of getting into trouble really frightens you, ask yourself why. Remember, you can be a good person even if you do something wrong from time to time.

146

Finding Your Voice

Five or more: Conflict is a fact of life and you're always willing to dare the possibility of social discord. You might say you're just being honest; others might call you a troublemaker. Balance is the goal you should keep in mind. Being able to assert yourself is a crucial skill, but make sure you're on the right side of the line between "asserting yourself" and "taking things out on people".

Four or fewer: You try to avoid conflict at all costs, which probably means you're pretty easy to get along with. But if you don't stand up and say what you think when it really matters, you're likely to wind up frustrated. You prefer to keep things gentle over having a heated argument, and that's admirable. The key here is knowing when breaking your silence is a risk worth taking.

Feeling the Emotion

Five or more: For you, feelings are an adventure. You put your passion to the test by exposing yourself to emotional extremes. Employing empathy can help deepen your understanding and compassion, but be careful not to get so caught up in other people's emotions that you avoid experiencing your own.

Four or fewer: You're not interested in other people's drama, but that doesn't mean you're cold to their feelings; you'd just rather see them happy. Or maybe you're focused on your own feelings and don't feel the need to pry.

Taking Your Chances

Five or more: You've got a gambling streak, haven't you? You're willing to "roll the dice" on something really great, no matter the risk. Gambling doesn't have to mean putting down money; when you engage in a project that may not pan out, or try a new friendship that could backfire, you're investing your time and energy for a "prize" that could slip out of reach. The trick here is knowing the odds: some things are worth betting on, but sometimes you need to cut your losses and move on.

Four or fewer: You prefer the safe way, choosing opportunities leading to predictably good benefits, rather than chancing a big loss for a possible big gain. You're reliable and consistent, which are two excellent qualities. If you find that you regret letting chances go by because you're too scared to try, though, you might want to up your game a bit.

CASTING CALL

The major motion picture of your life

The good news: we've got Hollywood on the line and they want to film your life story. The really good news: you're the casting director! Which actors and actresses will you cast in the key roles? Start by selecting who will play you, then decide who else will be in your story and which actors and actresses will play their parts.

THE LEAD (YOU!)
Played by:

SUPPORTING ROLE:

Played by:

SUPPORTING ROLE:

Played by:

ROLE:

Played by:

ROLE:

Played by:

ROLE:

Played by:

ROLE:

Played by:

ROLE:

Played by:

ROLE:

Played by:

ROLE:

Played by:

ROLE:

Played by:

ROLE:

Played by:

Nature's Palette

On page 22, you discovered the colour of your personality. Now find out what your favourite colour says about you and your relationship with nature.

Orange
is the colour of WARMTH.

Flames, sunsets, and flowers all have a glow about them. Think of fresh oranges and halloween lanterns lit by candlelight. Soft but strong, orange is associated with lightening darkness, like a bonfire against a night sky. To love orange is to love hope in adversity, to have faith there's always a light to follow.

Red
is the colour of VITALITY.

We associate it with danger – blood, alarms, stop signs. At the same time, it's intimate; no matter what we look like on the outside, under the skin, most of our body is some shade of red. It's a colour we associate with being at the "heart" of things, where we can find comfort. To love red is to love safety and danger as two sides of the same coin.

Green
is the colour of HARMONY.

Green is life to growing plants, the colour of leaves drinking in light and making the world lush. A day without green is a day without nature. It's in greenness that we find the world at its freshest and healthiest. In green, we find balance. To love green is to feel calm, to love and appreciate nature, and to respect our place in the world.

Yellow
is the colour of ENERGY.

No colour is more springy, whether it's newly hatched chicks or blossoming daffodils. A yellow room is fresh and cheerful on even the coldest day. There's something youthful about the colour yellow, a feeling of new beginnings and bright possibilities. To love yellow is to love rebirth, to believe that we don't need to hold ourselves back – that tomorrow may be even better than today.

Blue
is the colour of PEACE.

In the azure sky of a warm day or the indigo softness of a starry night, blue is always there, right above our heads, meeting us at every horizon. The blue water of seas and lakes is cleansing, giving the colour a healing touch. To love blue is to love natural beauty, to appreciate the knowledge that the world stretches out in all directions, offering us both comfort and limitless opportunities at the same time.

Purple
is the colour of SPIRIT.

From the grand purple of ancient emperors to the fading underbelly of a bright rainbow, purple is drama and grandeur, its vibrancy a glorious reminder of just how colourful the world can truly be. In purple we find joy and pride. To love purple is to love spectacular beauty, to know that in appreciation of both the world and ourselves lies true happiness.

Gold
is the colour of CELEBRATION.

In the gleam of gold metal we see sheer beauty for beauty's sake. You can make little that's practical out of gold, yet we love it all the same. Gold doesn't rust or corrode; its perfection is impervious to the worries of ordinary objects. To love gold is to love joy and to know that happiness is a prize well worth the finding.

Brown
is the colour of REALITY.

The earth under our feet holds us up with its brown solidity. The leaves in autumn turn brown in a cyclical reminder that all things renew themselves to thrive. Brown is a colour that comforts, reminding us of nourishing food and strong tree trunks. It's a colour we can depend on to be there for us. To love brown is to trust the world, to know that even the most everyday things are valuable.

White
is the colour of PURITY.

A colour so clean that only the most untouched of things can sustain it – from newly fallen snow to the fresh blossoms of a cherry tree – the fragility of white speaks of a state of pristine perfection, the world before time can touch it. To love white is to cherish the transient, to know that while nothing stays untarnished forever, that's all the more reason to love and enjoy it while it lasts.

Silver
is the colour of AWARENESS.

In the beauty of silver jewellery, and even the mundane silver knives and forks we handle every day, we see the heritage of human invention that's brought us to this day. To love silver is to love enlightenment, the glimmer of an active and intelligent mind, reflective and open to a wealth of possibilities.

Why do our favourite colours change over time?

Our colour preference is just one more way in which we talk to ourselves, telling ourselves how we feel in a language that helps us when we can't quite find the words. Have you reconsidered your values, or altered your perception of yourself? Has your life changed so you need more of one quality than another? What colours do you feel you need most right now?

my chore list

The desire to be independent can be complicated. You may be starting to feel more and more eager to stand on your own feet, but other people can send you mixed signals. You're often expected to be self-reliant and responsible, but at the same time, you're not fully trusted to do all things for yourself.

The road to independence is long and winding, and everyone walks at her own pace. Where are you on that road right now?

Circle one answer for each of the following questions.

1 THERE'S A NEW FILM OUT THAT YOU WANT TO SEE BUT YOUR FRIENDS DON'T. DO YOU:

A. Go alone; the point is to see the film and you don't need company for that.

B. Try to persuade them to join you, promising to do something they want to do afterwards.

C. Give up on the idea; you'll catch it when it comes out on DVD.

2 YOUR FAVOURITE TOP IS DIRTY, BUT YOU WANT TO WEAR IT TOMORROW. IT CAN BE MACHINE-WASHED, BUT NOT TUMBLE-DRIED. DO YOU:

A. Wash it with whatever other dirty clothes you have and promptly hang it up to dry.

B. Toss the top in the washing machine and hope you remember to unload it before someone else does.

C. Either ask your parents to clean the top for you, or wear it dirty.

3 A BIG TEST IS COMING UP IN A COUPLE OF WEEKS AND YOU NEED TO PREPARE. DO YOU:

A. Draw up a timetable, cancel other plans, and get yourself ready to study.

B. Talk to your friends and see if you can spend a few evenings revising together.

C. Organize a class study group so you can study together every evening.

4 YOU'RE ALONE IN THE HOUSE FOR THE EVENING, AND YOU'RE HUNGRY. DO YOU:

A. Cook yourself a proper meal and settle down to enjoy it.

B. Look through the fridge for leftovers or an easy-to-grab snack.

C. Stay hungry until someone gets home to cook supper for you.

5 YOU NEED TO GET YOUR HOMEWORK DONE, BUT YOU'RE STUCK ON A PROBLEM. DO YOU:

A. Read textbooks and articles online to see if you can work it out.

B. Call up your friends and ask if they're stuck as well.

C. Ask your parents to help; if they can't, leave the problem unfinished until you can ask your teacher about it.

6 YOUR FRIENDS ARE ALL AWAY FOR THE WEEKEND. DO YOU:

A. Keep yourself entertained doing stuff on your own.

B. Ask your family members if there's anything you could all do together.

C. Feel bored and count down the minutes until your friends return.

7 YOUR FAMILY IS OUT FOR THE EVENING AND THE POWER GOES OFF. DO YOU:

A. Find the torches and candles, and carry on with your evening.

B. Call one of your family members on their mobile and ask for advice.

C. Find your way upstairs in the dark and go to bed.

Now turn the page... >

For each "A" answer, give yourself 3 points.

For each "B" answer, give yourself 2 points.

For each "C" answer, give yourself 1 point.

Your total: ____

Score of 7–11:

Testing Your Wings

You're working on it, but independence is still pretty far away for you. It's good that there are people in your life you can rely on; hopefully this means your family members are dependable and your friends are great company. But you'll need to get some more skills under your belt before you're fully ready to fly. You may want to start gradually trying more and more things on your own so you feel confident in your abilities. Of course, some home and social environments make it easier to be independent than others; if your parents don't let you try stuff or your friends take offence if you don't do everything with them, you have to be much more assertive to get the same level of independence as someone in a more free-and-easy situation.

Score of 12–16:
One of the Group

You can manage on your own if you have to, but you still like to have some support from others. Given the choice, you'd rather do things with other people than act alone. Many people prefer a group setting and there are plenty of times when several heads are better than one. At the moment, you may be at the most sociable time of your life, and a lot of girls feel that almost everything is better done with friends. As long as you and your friends have a happy, healthy relationship, bonding with them can be a great foundation for the future. On the other hand, there are times when nobody else is around, so it's good to be able to do things alone if you really have to. As long as you're not actually incapable of doing things for yourself, there's nothing wrong with having a preference for working with other people; it's just a question of finding your comfort zone.

Score of 17–21:
Going It Alone

You're pretty much an adult when it comes to taking care of yourself. Some super-independent people were a little short on support when they were kids, forcing them to become independent fast. Others had plenty of support; they just love taking the reins and doing things their own way. Whichever camp you fall into, you're on top of things and know how to handle yourself. Just remember, there's a difference between being independent and being antisocial, and the fact that you can do things alone doesn't mean you have no other choice. It's okay to rely on others from time to time, especially when you find yourself in a difficult situation.

HIDDEN TALENTS

Some people are concert pianists or football stars, but talent doesn't have to be spectacular to be really cool. Even if you can't do a backflip, chances are there are a few things you can do that nobody else can, whether it's a funny voice, the world's best air guitar, or that weird thing you can do with your thumb. Fill in some of your hidden talents here.

What can you do?

....

....

....

Who knows about it?

....

When do you show it off?

....

....

What can you do?

....

....

Who knows about it?

....

When do you show it off?

....

....

What can you do?

....

....

Who knows about it?

....

When do you show it off?

....

....

Turn the page for more... >

< HIDDEN TALENTS

Give these tricks a try!

Tick the ones you complete.

- ◯ Wiggle your ears
- ◯ Cross your eyes
- ◯ "Cross" one eye and roll the other
- ◯ Roll your tongue
- ◯ "Cloverleaf" your tongue
- ◯ Touch your tongue to your nose
- ◯ Raise one eyebrow at a time
- ◯ Do an impression or funny voice
- ◯ Do the splits
- ◯ Draw a perfect circle without a stencil
- ◯ Recite a tongue twister super fast
- ◯ Balance a coin on your elbow then catch it in your palm
- ◯ Put your feet behind your head
- ◯ Twitch your nose
- ◯ Lick your own elbow
- ◯ Plait your own hair
- ◯ Gurn (crumple your mouth up under your nose)
- ◯ Sing an incredibly high or low note

" When you do the **common** things in life in an **uncommon** way, you will **command** the attention of the world. **"**

George Washington Carver

Made to be Broken

Sometimes it can seem like there's nothing but rules every way we look. Some of us like rules, feeling that having things clear makes it easier for everyone to get along happily. Some of us hate rules, finding them petty and restrictive, more about power than justice. Where do you stand?

1 Going for a swim, you pass a sign listing all the rules for poolside behaviour. Do you:

■ **A.** Read it in full. Every pool has its own rules and it's best to know what to expect.

■ **B.** Glance at it, but don't stop to read. It's not as if I was planning to do anything crazy anyway.

■ **C.** Read it to see if it's fair. If it's not, I'll discuss it with the management on the way out.

■ **D.** Check it out and if there's any rule I can break safely, I'll try to do it sneakily just for fun.

■ **E.** Ignore it and do what I want — when the lifeguard's not looking, at least!

2 You and your family are settling down to play a new board game. Do you:

■ **A.** Go through all the instructions and make sure everybody understands them.

■ **B.** Read enough to master the basics, then get started. We can always check again if we get stuck.

■ **C.** Jump right in. I'm more concerned about good sportsmanship from the players than what the rule book says.

■ **D.** Listen carefully as the rules are read — but only so I can find ways to get around them.

■ **E.** Hope the rules aren't too complicated. Let's keep it simple or play something else.

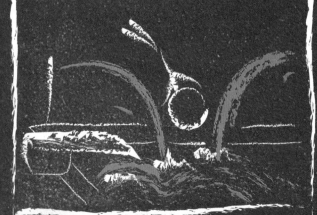

3 Your school dress code states that skirts can't be too short. Do you:

☐ **A.** Think that's fair enough: school's supposed to be for learning, after all.

☐ **B.** Not care very much: I've got enough outfits that will probably pass, so it's no big deal.

☐ **C.** Find other students who agree this is an infringement of freedom and circulate a petition.

☐ **D.** Wear my skirts exactly at the minimum length and enjoy watching teachers try to decide if I'm breaking the rule or not.

☐ **E.** Wear my skirts as short as possible, and only change if absolutely forced to.

4 While at a film, you find somebody's wallet with cash and cards in it under your seat. Do you:

☐ **A.** Take it to the staff right away – the person who lost it will need it back as soon as possible.

☐ **B.** Finish watching the film first and hand it in on my way out.

☐ **C.** Hand it in, pointing out to the management that the cleaning staff shouldn't have missed it.

☐ **D.** Slip something strange into the wallet, like a photo of your dog, just to confuse the owner.

☐ **E.** Hand it in, but take some money out of it first – hey, it's a finder's reward.

5 The local park closes at 10 p.m., but your friend wants to celebrate her birthday with a midnight picnic there. Do you:

☐ **A.** Feel uncomfortable about it. Maybe we could find a better location, like someone's garden?

☐ **B.** If that's what she wants, I'll do it, but we'd better not bring anything we can't pack in a hurry.

☐ **C.** Public places shouldn't close; I say we go and make a point of being safe just to prove it's okay.

☐ **D.** Say it sounds like a good idea and bring extra party hats to dress up the statues there.

☐ **E.** Look forward to unsupervised fun – what can we do there that our families wouldn't let us?

6 Your grumpy neighbour put a sign outside his house: "NO skateboarding on this street". Your little brother likes to skateboard. Do you:

☐ **A.** Suggest my brother plays further down the road – the bloke's a bit nuts, best not to annoy him.

☐ **B.** Ignore it: it's not worth getting upset and it's not like the guy can do anything to back it up.

☐ **C.** Call the council and ask them to give him a polite warning – he doesn't have the right to put up signs banning things.

☐ **D.** Sneak out and change it to "NO *banning* skateboarding on this street" with a big smiley face.

☐ **E.** Tear the sign down and if he comes out and shouts at me, I'll shout right back.

Turn the page for results... >

Made to be *Broken* Answers

Mostly As:
Good Citizen

Life is better for everyone when we all play fair: that's your motto. The way you see it, most rules are there for a reason. If we ignored them, nothing would work — so it's better to be considerate and trustworthy. Hopefully you wouldn't support a rule that's clearly bad, but all else being equal, you prefer to do things by the book. As long as you remain tolerant of people who are a little less "correct" than you, you're a dependable sort with your feet on solid ground.

Mostly Bs:
Peaceful Participant

You aren't planning to break the rules, but you're not going to let them dominate your life. As far as you're concerned, the main thing is to be a decent person. Rules are made by people and people are imperfect, so the best way to live is to judge each rule on a case-by-case basis. You know that some rules need to be bent. For you, using diplomacy is better than blindly following along.

Mostly Cs:
The Challenger

We need rules, but those rules need to be right. For you, the worst offence is abusing rules, not breaking them. Some people misuse their positions of power, and it's the vulnerable people who get the worst of it when that happens. Well, not on your watch: you'll speak up. You may not have a problem with authority as a concept, but you do think people need to be held accountable. When you rebel, you do it openly and cleanly, and for a clear reason.

> " Never, even as a child,
> # would I bend to a rule. "
> *Claude Monet*

> **"** I am slow-thinking and full of interior
>
> # rules that act as brakes
>
> on my desires...
>
> *F. Scott Fitzgerald, The Great Gatsby* **"**

Mostly Ds: Mischief Maker

Yeah, we probably need rules to get by, but they're stifling if we take them too literally. You don't want to be a criminal or an idiot, but if you can get a little fun out of bypassing authority, you're absolutely going to do it. It's important to you to keep things stirred up so we don't get stuck in a rut and forget to use our imaginations. You're hard to scare and you won't let rules take all the joy out of everything. A little spirit makes every rule more bearable.

Mostly Es: The Rebel

Life's for the living and rules are made to be broken. For you, authority is just another name for people throwing their weight around. You trust your own judgement and don't need anyone to tell you how to think. Try not to break rules just because they're there – that's the way to a life of more conflict than anyone can sustain. But your ability to think for yourself in the face of pressure can be valuable. Keep hold of your common sense and you'll be fine.

> **"** # Unheard-of
>
> combinations of circumstances demand
>
> # unheard-of rules. **"**
>
> *Charlotte Brontë, Jane Eyre*

WHAT
would you do?

Scenario 1

There's a friend of a friend who you often see at group events. Everyone else thinks he's a good guy, but you find him a little creepy.

Would you let your friends know you don't trust him?

. . . .

. . . .

If forced to talk to or interact with him, how would you do it?

. . . .

Imagine someone in your group notices that you seem to be avoiding the guy, and tells you you're being rude. What would you do?

. . . .

. . . .

. . . .

Scenario 2

Your best friend keeps making little comments about your clothes that hurt your feelings, but when you mention it, she says she's just joking.

Would you tell her she's upsetting you, or would you try to let it go?

. . . .

. . . .

If you decide to ignore or brush off her comments, how would you do it?

. . . .

If you tell her the comments bother you but she refuses to stop making them, would you end your friendship with her? Or would you grin and bear them? What would you do?

. . . .

. . . .

. . . .

Every now and then, we find ourselves in uncomfortable situations. They can range from a simple disagreement with a friend, to a big group pressuring you to do something you don't want to do, to a seriously dangerous encounter. How do you handle an uncomfortable situation and how good are you at getting yourself out of them? Do you trust yourself to make the right moves? Read the scenarios below and write your answers to the following questions.

Scenario 3

Two of your good friends are growing closer, and you're starting to feel like they're cutting you out of things, but they insist you're all still equal friends.

Would you talk to other friends about it?

....

How far would you go to keep your friendship with them?

....

....

If you tried to talk to them about the problem but they kept denying it, would you let it go? Would you try to find a new group of friends? What would you do?

....

....

....

Scenario 4

A teacher you don't get along with very well gives you a bad mark on your coursework, even though you worked really hard and thought you did a good job.

Would you feel comfortable talking to the teacher about the mark?

....

Would you question whether or not your coursework was actually any good?

....

....

If you tried to talk to your teacher about the mark but she refused to discuss it, would you tell your family? Would you go to the headteacher? What would you do?

....

....

....

Turn the page for more... >

< WHAT
would you do?

Scenario 5

A friend shows up at your house and asks you to go with her to steal a street sign. You think it's a bad idea, but she's insisting it will be fun.

Would you go along with her even if your instincts told you not to?

. . . .

. . . .

Would you try to talk her out of it?

. . . .

. . . .

If you decided not to go with her, would you tell someone about her plan? Would you let her go through with it without telling anyone? What would you do?

. . . .

. . . .

. . . .

Scenario 6

A close friend who you've known for a long time asks you on a date – but you're not interested in a romantic relationship with that person.

Would you feel uncomfortable around that person when you saw them next?

. . . .

. . . .

Would you tell your other friends that this person asked you on a date?

. . . .

Would you agree to the date just to make your friend happy? Or would you let them down gently? What would you do?

. . . .

. . . .

. . . .

What would you do in these uncomfortable scenarios? Read them alone and think about your answers, or take turns reading them aloud with friends and discussing your reactions.

You got a poor mark on a test and your parents want to talk to you about it. How would you handle it?

You and your best friend have a crush on the same person. What would you do?

You get paired up with a person you don't like very much as your lab partner, and the person suggests going to your house to study. What would you say?

You forget to show up for a shift at work and your boss asks you to explain yourself. What would you say?

You get caught sneaking out at night and your parents are angry. What would you do?

You show up to a school dance wearing the same dress as someone else, and she asks you to go home and change. Would you do it?

You're asked to a party by a classmate who is really nice, but you'd rather go with someone else. What would you say?

Your best friend tells you she wants to hang out less, but she won't tell you why. What would you do?

You're at a friend's house for supper and her mum is serving a dish you really don't like. Would you say something?

It's the little things

There are plenty of big events to deal with, like holidays, your school leaver's dance, turning sixteen... It's so easy to get so caught up in these momentous occasions that we forget most of our lives are made up of little moments – and those little moments can add up to something pretty wonderful.

Here's a challenge: For one full day, make an effort to notice the little moments. List here every nice, kind, honest, or impressive act you witness by the people around you.

....

....

....

....

....

....

....

....

....

....

Bonus Challenge: Pass it on. After seeing the good things going on around you, are you inspired to go out and do good for others? How will you keep the good vibes going strong?

"No act of kindness, no matter how small, is ever wasted."

Aesop

Sweet Charity

One for all and all for one.

However individual we are, we're all in it together on this complicated planet and most of us like to do things that make life better for our fellow planet-dwellers. Given infinite time and resources, there are probably a million good causes we'd each like to help, but realistically, we often have to pick just a few that we feel most passionately about. The charities and causes we prioritize say a lot about our ideals and values. What do yours say about you?

TAKE A LOOK AT THIS CHECKLIST AND CHECK OFF THE FIVE CAUSES THAT YOU FIND THE MOST INSPIRING, URGENT, OR IMPORTANT.

- The environment
- Human rights
- Helping the homeless
- Researching cures for diseases
- Caring for the sick
- Social and political justice
- Feeding the hungry
- Disaster relief
- Helping abused children
- Support for disabled people
- Animal welfare
- Preserving cultural treasures
- Protecting endangered species

- Supporting the developing world
- Helping soldiers and military families
- Clean water
- Rescue and lifeboat organizations
- Educational outreach
- International medical aid
- Helping domestic violence victims
- Preserving the rainforests
- Counselling for people in distress
- Community organizing
- Organ donation
- Creating opportunities for disadvantaged people

What can YOU do to help?

We all have different talents for helping our favourite causes. Check off the **five statements** below that are most true of you, then read on to find out more.

"I like using my **hobbies and talents for a good cause.**"

"I feel **wonderful** when I stand up to **injustice.**"

"I'm a good **communicator.**"

"I love making **new friends.**"

"I can get a great project **moving.**"

"I don't mind **hard work** if it's important."

"I love meeting **new people.**"

"I'm pretty **organized and reliable.**"

"I'm not shy to ask for **money.**"

"I take on **new challenges with courage.**"

"I can be **tactful and persuasive.**"

"I love to get **hands-on.**"

Mostly RED:
Charities can't do anything without money, and for that, they need people willing to put themselves out there and raise it. From the sound of it, you're one of those people. Whether it's getting sponsorship for doing something by yourself, or helping set up a big team event, you can get the cash – the lifeblood of any cause – flowing in.

Mostly BLUE:
Most problems don't go away just because we ask them nicely, and at that point, we need people to raise the banners or man the barricades. You are passionate and have a courageous streak; you're not afraid of meeting injustice head-on, and you can be brave when you have to be. Activism may be calling to you!

Mostly GREEN:
Some causes need organization on a huge scale, far more than any one person can manage. For that, they need good soldiers ready to make calls, knock on doors, post on sites, and get the grassroots flourishing. This kind of charity is definitely marathon rather than sprint, but it's people like you who move mountains in the end.

Mostly PURPLE:
If charity begins at home, your idea of home doesn't stop at your front door. For you, a great idea may be getting out into your local area, whether it's volunteering at a youth centre or cleaning up a local river. People on the ground like you can touch lives and make a whole community a healthier, happier, and more wonderful place to be.

Under pressure

There's no denying it.

Being a teenager is stressful. Between the hormonal cocktail that your brain's throwing at itself every day, the pressure to act as responsible as an adult and as compliant as a child at the same time, the constant demands to do well and think of your future, the day-to-day dramas of friendship and family... well, it's amazing you haven't driven yourself nuts.

Take a deep breath. You can't totally avoid all of the stress in your life – but once you have a handle on what gets you worked up, you can find ways to control it.

WHAT ARE THE BIGGEST STRESSES IN YOUR LIFE?

> ## "It's hard to take all of the responsibility and keep such a tight timetable. "
>
> Gabrielle, 18

WHEN AND HOW OFTEN DO YOU FEEL STRESSED? (ALL OF THE TIME, SOMETIMES, ALMOST NEVER...)

WHAT DO YOU DO WHEN YOU'RE FEELING REALLY STRESSED OUT?

WHO ARE THE PEOPLE YOU TRUST TO GET YOU THROUGH A STRESSFUL SITUATION?

Turn the page for more info...

Under pressure

< Stress management

When our brains receive stress signals, we can start getting a panicky feeling. Our memory, impulse control, concentration, and ability to learn all plummet when we're feeling that pressure. Basically, we have a lot more trouble thinking straight when we're stressed. If life is getting on top of you and you need to get your bearings, try one of these stress-management techniques to get you through.

EXERCISE: Even moderate exercise has a powerful antidepressant and anti-anxiety effect. Plus, feeling healthy never made anyone feel worse...

"THE TALKING CURE": Feeling supported by others can be calming, and talking things out can help you organize your thoughts.

BEING GENEROUS: One way to feel our own strength is to do something for somebody else. Experiencing oneself as a giver can really cut down the helpless feelings.

Different people have different methods of dealing with stress. Which of these techniques work best for you? What other techniques do you use to keep cool when you're stressed out?

❝ The hardest part about being a teenager is dealing with all of the stresses of life. ❞
Alex, 16

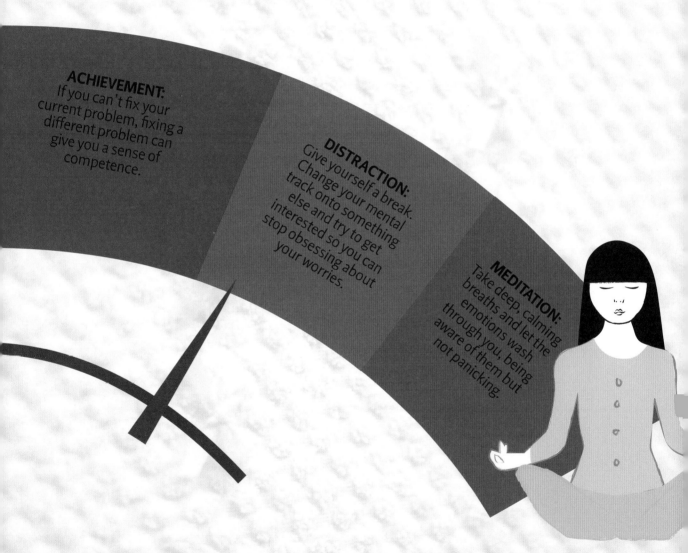

ACHIEVEMENT:
If you can't fix your current problem, fixing a different problem can give you a sense of competence.

DISTRACTION:
Give yourself a break. Change your mental track onto something else and try to get interested so you can stop obsessing about your worries.

MEDITATION:
Take deep, calming breaths and let the emotions wash through you, being aware of them but not panicking.

❝ Being a teenager is like people telling you 'juggle this' before you've learned how to juggle. ❞
Lauren, 14

Me & the Media

Bombarding the senses

We live in a world where it's hard (nearly impossible, really) to escape the media. Even just walking down the street, chances are we'll overhear car radios, pass billboards and posters, see company logos on people's coffee cups and clothes...

Most of us get used to tuning out the media overload, keeping our focus on what we actually want to consume. But whether we acknowledge it or not, the adverts we ignore and flyers we only glance at still hit our eyes and brain – so it can be telling to take some time to work out just how much information there really is surrounding us.

TRY THIS: For a full day, record all the media you consume, whether by choice or as a bystander. Include TV, books, films, music, Internet, advertising and branding, radio, newspapers, and anything else you notice.

Turn the page for more space to write...

At the end of the day, are you surprised by how much media you encountered? How do you sort out your priorities in its midst?

DEALING WITH
MEDIA OVERLOAD?

Here's some expert advice.

DON'T

Spend your time consuming media that makes you feel insecure or unworthy.

Engage in media that offers a hateful or mean-spirited message.

Use your camera or video recorder so often that you miss out on having in-the-moment experiences.

Be afraid to leave your smartphone or tablet at home once in a while. It can be freeing to disconnect now and then.

Feel pressured to change your mindset based on what a piece of media tells you.

DO

Look critically at information ads or commercials give you.

Understand that media doesn't often give objective advice – it's designed to get you to hand over your cash or think a certain way.

Take time to decide whether or not you agree with what you're reading.

Know your own philosophies and beliefs.

Monitor how much media you expose yourself to and how that makes you feel.

Manage the amount of time you spend on social networks each day, especially if you feel you're overusing them or are "addicted" to them.

If you're feeling overwhelmed by media, try a cleanse: go camping, take a media-free walk in the park, or have a good conversation with a friend.

Work of Art

Standing the test of time

After history is forgotten and cultures are lost, what lasts is the art that people create. Art is one of the most powerful ways humans express their individuality and their independence. We will never stop finding new ways to express ourselves and push our artistic boundaries to the limit.

1 WHAT ART FORMS DO YOU USE TO EXPRESS YOURSELF?

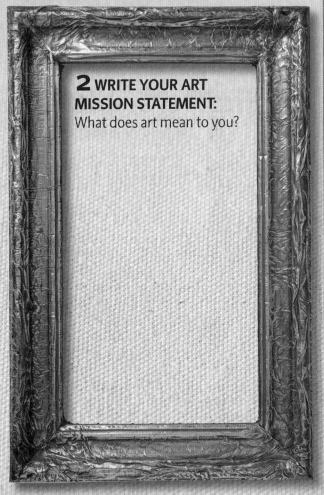

2 WRITE YOUR ART MISSION STATEMENT:
What does art mean to you?

3 LOOK UP THESE FAMOUS PAINTINGS ONLINE OR IN AN ART ANTHOLOGY.
What words or feelings come to mind when you look at them?

Johannes Vermeer's "Girl With A Pearl Earring"

Vincent Van Gogh's "Starry Night"

Edvard Munch's "The Scream"

Gustav Klimt's "The Kiss"

Edgar Degas's "The Dancing Class"

Georgia O'Keeffe's "Blue and Green Music"

Jackson Pollock's "Number 11, 1952"

Use this space to create your own work of art.
You can draw or paint, stick in photographs or pictures
from magazines, write a poem, draft song lyrics...
Express yourself through any medium you choose.

Seeing the Future

What's out there for you?

Is the future a mountain you can't wait to scale, a winding path you're curious to walk, or a foggy landscape you're not so eager to stumble into?

We're always being told to plan for the future, and some of us are better at it than others, but for many, planning long-term can feel next to impossible. How can you know what you want in five years time when you don't know for sure what you'll want in five weeks?

Take this quiz to help you gather your thoughts.

Pick one answer for each question to find out your feelings about the future.

Think back three or four years. Are you now where you thought you'd be then?

A. Pretty much, I'm happy to say.

B. Pretty much. I don't feel so much happy as resigned, though.

C. Not at all. I was a totally different person than I am now!

D. Honestly, I'm not sure. I didn't really know what to expect back then.

Someone asks you that "Where do you see yourself in ten years?" question. Do you:

A. Have a clear plan laid out that I'm happy to discuss. Maybe they'll have some good advice.

B. Tell them my plan, but quickly; I'm really tired of talking about it.

C. Raise several possibilities – a lot can happen in ten years.

D. Want to change the subject. I don't have a plan and I don't like being asked about it.

You have to volunteer for a community outreach or charity project. What do you pick?

A. Something productive that'll give me skills I can use in my long-term goals.

B. Something exciting that gives me a chance to try something new.

C. Something social that gets me out meeting interesting people.

D. Something meaningful that reflects my deepest personal passions and values.

When you daydream, do your future plans play a part in some of them?

A. Yes: I've got a dream and I love to picture myself succeeding at it.

B. I more often daydream to escape thoughts of the future, really.

C. Sometimes; I like to try on different possibilities and see how they appeal.

D. Not usually; my daydreams are for other things.

How do you feel about the words *fate* and *destiny*?

A. They're something I want to be the master of.

B. They sound sort of depressing.

C. They sound exciting, but I don't take them too seriously.

D. It'd be nice to have a destiny. I wish life was that simple.

You're offered an opportunity that sounds good but would take you in an unexpected direction. Do you:

A. Regretfully turn it down. I've got my eyes on the prize and I know what I want most.

B. Jump at the chance and hope I don't meet opposition from family and friends.

C. Give it a try and see how it pans out.

D. Take it with great relief: an unexpected direction is better than no direction!

It's career day at school and there are people from different walks of life there to give advice. Do you:

A. Zero in on the person who can help me most and ask them what they'd recommend.

B. Dutifully talk to the right people, but not really enjoy it.

C. Chat with whoever seems interesting.

D. Wander around and listen to everyone randomly.

Now turn the page...

What do your answers show?

Mostly A:

You know what you're about, that's for sure! You have a dream and, more than that, you enjoy thinking about how to reach it: your life is pointing in a single direction and that's how you want it. For you, aspiration is a pleasure and plans blend nicely with a sense of anticipation for a great future.

Best-case scenario: You have a vocation that you spend your life pursuing, and by the time you're done, you can look back with true satisfaction on time well spent. Perhaps your success will be amazing and world-shaking; perhaps it'll just be quietly pleasing. Either way, you made your choice, you lived it, and you feel sure it was the right choice to make.

Worst-case scenario: You dedicate your life to a single goal and it doesn't pan out, leaving you feeling like a failure. To guard against this, make sure that however central to your life your dream is, it's not the only thing capable of making you happy or giving you meaning. Other sources of joy and support can only enrich your later successes, and they can make the difference between wisdom and bitterness if you encounter any bad luck.

Mostly B:

Somebody's got your life planned out, but is that somebody you? Some of us choose our own dreams, but others have to deal with external pressures: ambitious families, difficult circumstances we need to get out of, limited options, anxiety about pursuing the more desirable long shots. You know where you're going, but it doesn't sound like you're all that excited about it.

Best-case scenario: You stick to your goals, creating meaning and satisfaction in them as you go, and come to terms with your decisions, making a success of it and becoming contented and wise. Alternatively, you discover a side alley branching off from your path, follow it, and find yourself in a much better place than you expected.

Worst-case scenario: You follow the route laid down for you, but you never really enjoy it. If it doesn't go well, you end up frustrated and regretful that you gave up the chance of a more interesting path for so little reward. If it does go well, things are okay, but you never lose that nagging sense that there must be more to life than this.

Mostly C:

You're not so much worried about the future as curious about it; it could hold any number of exciting possibilities. Most likely you have talents in several areas and are in no hurry to settle down to just one, knowing that each choice has its own advantages and suspecting that fixing on any option means giving up on others.

Best-case scenario: You learn from everything you try, becoming a dynamic and well-rounded person who combines her skills into a success all the richer for having a wide variety of experience behind it. Life may have its rocky patches, but nothing is wasted, and in the end you wouldn't have missed any of it.

Worst-case scenario: You dissipate your energy into different projects that don't add up to very much, always knowing you could do great things but never managing to stick to anything long enough to make it happen. In the end, life looks disappointing and full of missed opportunities. To guard against this, make yourself promises that you'll never give up on a project until you've given it a realistic amount of time to work – or at least, to gain some transferable skills.

Mostly D:

How are you supposed to know what you want when you still aren't sure who you are? For you, being loaded down with decisions this huge is just not something you're ready for; it's all a bit overwhelming and you need some breathing space. Possibly you have some dreams but they seem unrealistic, or else you just need your own time.

Best-case scenario: As you try things, you start to discover your strengths and talents, gradually building towards a future that's all the better for being chosen from a position of experience. You start to see realistic ways to pursue your real dreams and make them come true, living a life that's both flexible and fulfilling.

Worst-case scenario: You accept whatever seems most doable to save yourself from having to make a decision, and get stuck on a path that you don't like but can't find a way off. You know you're not happy, but you don't feel able to work out how to do whatever's necessary to make things better. To guard against this, be careful of the easy option and make time, if only in private, to work on things you care about, however farfetched they may seem.

Dear Future Me...

Use this space to write a letter to your future self. What do you hope she's accomplished? What do you want to remind her about? What should she never forget?

"I am not afraid of storms, for I am learning how to sail my ship."

LOUISA MAY ALCOTT,
LITTLE WOMEN

Acknowledgements

The publishers would like to thank the following people for their help in the creation of this book: Joannah Ginsburg for her insight and guidance; Nancy Ellwood for editorial acumen and awesomeness; Martha Burley for editorial help and guidance; Kate Fenton and Rose Frankland for illustrations; Jennifer Chung and Sarah Tibbling for editorial assistance; Darren Baldwin for photographs in the top left, top right, and bottom left corners of page 14; Lindsay Walter for proofreading; Elizabeth Yeates and Harriet Yeomans for help in the book's early stages; Rosie Chen for her help; our survey takers – Alex, Cameron, Gabrielle, Imogen, Jennifer, Kath, Kay, Laura-Alice, Lauren, Mina, Molly, Natalie, Nicolette, and Sarah; and our lunchtime quiz testers – Kimberly, Sarah, Jennifer, Kristen, and Kell.

Thank you!